*Calochortus
kennedyi*

the National Wildflower Research Center's
Wildflower Handbook

Penstemon palmeri

A Resource for Native Plant Landscapes,
Second Edition

the National Wildflower Research Center's

Wildflower Handbook

Delphinium nuttallianum

A Resource for Native Plant Landscapes, *Second Edition*

❖

Royalties from the sale of the *Wildflower Handbook* benefit the
NATIONAL WILDFLOWER RESEARCH CENTER

published by
VOYAGEUR PRESS

Text copyright © 1992 by the National Wildflower Research Center
2600 FM 973 North
Austin, Texas 78725
(512)929-3600

❖

Printed in the United States of America
92 93 94 95 96 5 4 3 2 1

Cover design and illustration, and interior illustrations, by Mary Welborn Davis
Book designed by Helene Jones

Library of Congress Cataloging-in-Publication Data available

ISBN 0-89658-201-9

Published by
VOYAGEUR PRESS, INC.
P.O. Box 338, 123 North Second Street
Stillwater, MN 55082 U.S.A.
From Minnesota and Canada 612-430-2210
Toll-free 800-888-9653

Voyageur Press books are also available at discounts for quantities for educational, fundraising, premium, or sales-promotion use. For details contact the
marketing department. Please write or call for our free catalog of natural history
publications and our free newsletter, *Wingbeat*.

CONTENTS

the National Wildflower Research Center's

Wildflower Handbook

A Resource for Native Plant Landscapes,
Second Edition

A critical problem facing the earth and its inhabitants is the ecological imbalance caused by the loss of native flora.

The National Wildflower Research Center was created in 1982 by Lady Bird Johnson to encourage a legacy of natural beauty and ecological stability, and to foster a desirable environment for future generations.

The Wildflower Center is a research and educational organization committed to the preservation and reestablishment of native wildflowers, grasses, shrubs, and trees.

The National Wildflower Research Center is a 501(C)3 non-profit organization governed by a national volunteer Board of Trustees and operated by a professional staff located in Austin, Texas. Financial support is provided by individual, foundation, and corporate grants and donations, and membership dues.

NATIONAL WILDFLOWER RESEARCH CENTER
2600 FM 973 North
Austin, Texas 78725-4201
(512)929-3600

Caltha
palustris

Acknowledgments

Editors:
Elizabeth S. Anderson
Annie Paulson Gillespie

Managing Editor:
Tela Goodwin Mange

Staff Contributors:
John E. Averett
Elinor Crank
Alison Hill
Kathryn Kramer McKinney
David K. Northington
Maria Urice

Volunteer Support:
Mary Hovden
Jeanne Richardson
Betty Ripperger
Jane Tillman

Information for this handbook has been accumulated over several years and is continuously updated. We thank those companies, organizations, and individuals who have responded to our questionnaires. We also must recognize past staff members and volunteers who were involved in the early stages of this project, and all current staff members who helped with various phases of the project.

Special acknowledgment is due the members of the National Wildflower Research Center's Board of Trustees who have served on the Research Committee and the Publications Committee.

Co-chairs of the National Wildflower Research Center Board:
Lady Bird Johnson and Helen Hayes

President:
Dana Leavitt

Past-President:
Nash Castro

Sarracenia minor

Introduction

The National Wildflower Research Center is a non-profit organization dedicated to the conservation of North American flora and the reestablishment of plants native to particular regions. Our natural plant communities have been diminished and significantly altered by the loss of native plants and animals and by the addition of naturalized, often aggressive, non-native plants. The loss of those plants and their associated species, besides leading to species extinction, removes much of the genetic diversity from such populations and can create erosion problems. Through research and education, the Wildflower Center strives to help others to understand the ecological, economic, and aesthetic benefits of native plants and to facilitate their preservation and reestablishment.

A primary objective of the Center is to provide appropriate information about native wildflowers, grasses, trees, and shrubs so that every individual can participate in the conservation and reestablishment of our native flora at all levels—from home gardens to large natural areas.

In particular, the Center emphasizes the use of *native, indigenous* plants (those that were found naturally in any given region before European settlement). Such plants have become adapted, over thousands of years, to survive extremes in temperature and rainfall and are well-suited to local soils and the associated plants and microorganisms of their regions. Some plants from other parts of the country or the world, such as Queen Anne's lace and chicory, have escaped cultivation and become *naturalized* (able to live successfully in the wild). While the Center does not necessarily advocate the removal of such species, except for those that are especially trouble-some, we do not encourage planting those species as "wildflowers," because of their tendencies to spread and crowd out native species. Some naturalized species, such as kudzu and purple loosestrife, have proven to be real ecological problems and, if possible, should be controlled or removed.

Although native landscapes require careful planning and man-agement, and considerable care during the first few years, the long-term benefits—lower maintenance, reduced need for chemicals, reduced water use, and increased wildlife habitat, to name a few—make the initial efforts more than worthwhile.

This handbook outlines basic considerations and procedures for adding native plants to your landscape, and provides lists of resources for each state including native plant nurseries and seed companies; botanic gardens, arboreta, nature centers with native plant displays, other conservation organizations and governmental agencies that work with native plants; and landscape architects and designers who use native plants for more ecologically based, environmentally sensitive landscapes. A glossary of definitions is provided on page 31.

WHY LANDSCAPE WITH NATIVE PLANTS?

Increased public awareness of environmental issues and problems in the 1980s led many to declare the 1990s as the "Decade of the Environment." Toxic pesticides and water shortages have become household concerns across the country, while Xeriscape, prairie restoration, and endangered species are common topics in the daily news. Planting "native" may become as popular as buying "green" products, as more people realize that native plants are an integral part, if not the basis, of the solution to those problems—ecologically, economically, and aesthetically.

Reestablishing native species in urban and rural areas adds to a patchwork of habitats for wildlife, and helps to link larger natural areas. Such plantings offer refuges and seed banks for wild species decimated by development and agriculture. (For more information on wildlife gardening, please see page 53.)

By planting native species, moreover, you encourage the presence of native insects and microorganisms that benefit the plants and keep them healthy without the use of chemical fertilizers and pesticides.

For homeowners in areas suffering from drought or subject to water rationing, native plants provide an opportunity to create attractive regional landscapes that can survive on rainfall.

As you begin experimenting with native plants, you'll become more aware of the plants' needs, and their interactions with other species and the environment. Your landscape will become an interacting, changing entity rather than a fixed object—offering a glimpse of the complexities of the natural world in your own backyard.

Liatris
pycnostachya

Adding Native
Plants to Your Landscape

Before incorporating native species into your landscape, you need to learn about the plants and soils of your area. Most parts of the country have one or more books about local flora (plants that are native to any given region) to use as references. Armed with those resources, you can explore natural areas and observe the plants in their habitats. Identifying the environmental conditions that favor different plants, as well as taking note of their bloom periods and duration, growth habits, and associated species, will help you to decide which species you like and which would do well on your site. The key to successfully using native plants in your landscape is selecting plants that fit your soil, moisture, and sunlight conditions.

Visiting botanic gardens, nature centers, and arboreta that have native plant displays is another good way to learn the local flora and see various combinations of native species growing together. (See the list of information sources on page 61 for local resources.) Native plant nursery personnel usually can advise you on cultivation tips and ideal growing conditions for the plants they sell. Once you feel reasonably familiar with your area's plants, you're ready to start experimenting.

Starting Out

How you incorporate native plants into your landscape depends on what is present and what you want to do with the landscape.

If you're building a new home, save as many of the existing native species as possible. Putting temporary fencing around trees and shrubs to protect them during construction is well worth the added costs.

Stockpile any soil that must be moved or disturbed. Native soil contains myriad microorganisms that are essential for healthy plants, as well as a storehouse of seeds from past years. Try to remove the soil layers in units, keeping the topsoil separate from subsoil layers.

You may even want to wait to see what comes up before adding or changing anything on your site. Once you assess what is on your property, you can begin to enhance or alter areas for improvement. It helps to make a landscape plan before grabbing a shovel. Mapping the soil types, pH, exposure differences, and moisture availability will help you later in selecting plants for various sections of your yard.

If, like most people, your landscape is already in place, a variety of options for incorporating native species exist, depending on the time and money you wish to invest, and the end result you envision. The easiest way to add native plants and wildflowers is to gradually replace non-natives with appropriate native species in places where the non-natives have died or are growing poorly. Create a master plan first and fill in the design as circumstance allows.

Reassess your lawn areas; consider reducing their size by creating a wildflower meadow or mulched beds with native plants. Limiting turf will cut down labor, water, and chemical costs. Rocks and gravel offer additional uses as mulch or elements for landscape design.

As with traditional landscape design, think about characteristics such as height, bloom period, color, texture, and growth habit when selecting plants, and group the plants accordingly. When planted in garden beds, native species often become much larger and bloom longer than they do in the wild because of increased nutrients and moisture and less competition. Colorscaping—choosing species for year-round color—is another aspect to consider when selecting plants for your landscape. Native bunch grasses make excellent accent plants, while plants with unusual foliage can be just as attractive as blossoms.

Once you begin experimenting with native plants, you may want to go one step further and mimic natural plant communities by planting species in associations as they occur in nature. Even a small yard can include a variety of habitats, such as open meadows, wooded areas, and perhaps a small wetland or seepage zone.

"Restoration landscaping" reassembles the plant species of the community that were (or might have been) native to the project site, in an effort to restore its natural functions and processes. This level of complexity requires considerable expertise to reconstruct and usually entails long-term (two to three years minimum) management. Wild-seed harvesting is frequently the best source of suitable plant propagules, and restorationists may chose to use plant succession as one tool to achieve a biological diversity that approaches a natural ecosystem. Severely disturbed sites may require intensive labor, but this type of landscaping also yields the maximum impact when the goals are improving the environment, adding to the patchwork of habitat, and increasing fragments of ecosystems.

Obtaining Native Plants and Seeds

The number of nurseries carrying or specializing in native plants and seeds has increased dramatically over the past five years. (See page 147 in this handbook for commercial sources in your area.) Always buy *nursery-propagated* plants, rather than wild-dug plants, so you don't contribute to the destruction of natural populations by commercial exploitation. Nursery-propagated plants, moreover, already will have compact, well-developed root systems and the hardiness to withstand transplanting.

Don't hesitate to ask nursery personnel the origin of their plant materials if you're skeptical. Be especially wary of buying woodland plants in the lily family, such as trilliums (*Trillium* spp.), trout lilies (*Erythronium* spp.), Solomon's seal (*Polygonatum* spp.), wild lilies (*Lilium* spp.), and bellworts (*Uvularia* spp.). Wild-collected orchids often include lady's slippers (*Cypripedium* spp.), orchis (*Orchis* spp.), and rattlesnake plantain (*Goodyera* spp.). Other species to be careful of are wild irises (*Iris* spp.), jack-in-the-pulpit (*Arisaema triphyllum*), Dutchman's breeches (*Dicentra cucullaria*), and shooting stars (*Dodecatheon* spp.) (Scott, 1986; Campbell, 1988). Other bulb plants, ferns, cacti, and succulents have been depleted in the wild in some areas.

Many of these species are difficult (if not impossible at this time) to propagate, and may take many years to grow to a marketable size. The listed price is a good indicator of whether one of these hard-to-grow plants has been propagated. If the price is low, chances are the plant has been dug from the wild (Scott, 1986; Brumback, 1988).

Besides disturbing natural populations, transplanting may not even be successful for many of those species, because of their highly specific growing conditions and mycorrhizal (soil fungus-root) associations. Some plants you just have to enjoy in their natural habitats! (The only acceptable instance for digging from the wild, given permission, is when the area is about to be developed.) To combat wild-collection problems, encourage your local suppliers to carry only nursery-propagated plants.

As you learn more about native plants, you may wish to collect seeds from wild plants. When done conservatively and conscientiously, wild-seed harvesting is a good way to increase species diversity and obtain more obscure species that are not available through commercial growers. (For more details on collecting seeds, see page 35.)

Wildflower Mixes

When buying seeds, think twice before purchasing a "wildflower" mix. For a variety of reasons, the Wildflower Center does not recommend mixes. In most cases, it is difficult to determine the composition of a mix, both for the individual species and their relative contributions. Such mixes often contain a high percentage of species outside their natural ranges. Be sure to check the list of seeds contained in the mix and find out if they are native to your area before purchasing! Generally, you are better off buying individual native wildflower seeds and planting them individually or making your own mix. (For more details on buying wildflower seeds in bulk, please see page 43.)

PLANTING A WILDFLOWER MEADOW

Much of the recent interest and enthusiasm about wildflowers and native plants revolves around the creation of wildflower meadows as alternative lawns. Although the definition varies, a meadow generally is a mixture of grasses and flowers growing in sunny, open fields or forest clearings. Meadows occur extensively in areas such as prairies and mountains, where environmental factors limit the growth of woody species and check the natural process of plant succession. Most meadows are temporary, however, and eventually will be invaded and replaced by shrubs and trees, so long-term management is vital in maintaining a meadow.

Native grasses are an essential element of wildflower meadows. Most people who manage meadows and prairies recommend that native grasses comprise 50 to 80 percent of the species composition. Grasses have several functions:

✓ to provide support and protection for tall flowers,

✓ to fill in spaces around wildflowers otherwise occupied by weeds,
✓ to add color and texture,
✓ to control erosion, and
✓ to act as a food source for wildlife.

Grasses typically exhibit one of two characteristic growth forms: sod-forming or bunch-forming. Sod grasses spread by runners or stolons (stems that grow horizontally along the ground and put down roots). Bunch grasses grow in distinct clumps.

Many native sod grasses, such as buffalograss (*Buchloe dactyloides*), grow in a loose matrix that easily allows room for wildflowers. Open spaces between native bunch grasses, such as bluestems (*Andropogon* spp.), grama grasses (*Bouteloua* spp.), and muhly grasses (*Muhlenbergia* spp.), also provide gaps for herbaceous plants to become established.

Conversely, many non-native turf grasses, such as St. Augustine and annual rye, are too thick or competitive to allow other plants to become established. In addition, many of those turf grasses are cool-season grasses, which grow concurrently with spring wildflowers and compete with them for water and nutrients.

Cool-season grasses begin to grow in early spring, with maximum development in late March to early June. They reach maturity and produce seeds in late spring to early summer, and become semi-dormant as summer heat increases. Growth usually resumes during the cool months of fall, and in southern latitudes, cool-season grasses remain green even after a frost.

Warm-season grasses resume their growth in late spring and continue growing until early fall, producing most of their foliage in mid-summer. Their growth periods do not compete with wildflower seed germination and establishment in the South; and as long as the proportion of grass-to-wildflower seeds is compatible, competition with warm-season grasses should not be a problem for wildflowers in the North.

Selecting and Preparing a Site

It's best to experiment with a wildflower meadow on a small scale at first. You can always add to the planting once you've determined which species are best suited to your site and fine-tuned your planting techniques. The amount of ground preparation you need to do depends on what's already on the site and whether the soil is natural, disturbed, or foreign, and how you eventually want it to look.

If your site is not particularly weedy and you plan only to interseed wildflowers into existing vegetation, the process is fairly straightforward. Before planting, mow the vegetation as short as possible, and rake off the thatch. Try to open up some bare areas so that the seeds will fall directly onto the soil. You must have good soil-seed contact for seeds to germinate and grow.

If your site is full of weeds, killing them may take a year or more. It is always easier and often less expensive to eliminate weeds before planting, rather than trying to control them in a newly seeded site. (Removing all of the weeds may not even be feasible on an extremely disturbed site.) Clear the area by repeated shallow tilling (no deeper than one inch) and watering, or application of an herbicide. The number of repetitions needed depends on the size of the area, the aggressiveness of the existing weeds, and the degree of weed control you desire. Weed seeds, roots, and rhizomes frequently lie dormant beneath the soil surface, and germinate quickly after they are exposed to moisture and light. The less you disturb the area, the easier it will be to control the weeds.

If you prefer not to till or hand-weed, two applications of a non-residual herbicide such as Roundup may be sufficient to remove existing vegetation. Before you apply Roundup, water the site for a week or two to promote germination of weed seeds. Allow the new seedlings to grow for one to two weeks, then apply Roundup as the label specifies, and only on a windless day. Wick applicators provide better control of application than sprayers. Repeat this process once more to ensure a fairly clean seed bed. Because it is not residual,

Roundup does not continue its herbicidal activity in the soil and you can plant wildflower and native grass seeds as soon as you are sure competing vegetation is under control. Roundup will not affect germinating seeds, only the growing plants that you have treated.

When to Plant

Planting time depends on where you live and what species you'll be planting. Fall is the best time to plant many native seeds. Some seeds need a chilling period (cold stratification) to break their dormancy. Others have hard seed coats that need to be worn down or scarified before the seeds can germinate. Sowing seeds in the fall often provides the conditions necessary to break seed dormancy. Warm, wet spring weather then induces the seeds to germinate. (For more details on seed propagation, see page 49.)

Wildflower seeds should be planted in the fall (September and October) in southern states. Southern annuals germinate in early fall, in response to rainfall, and overwinter as seedlings. By developing good root systems and low, ground-hugging forms, the seedlings can protect themselves from cold winter temperatures. Planting native perennials in the fall helps break seed dormancy. Cool-season grasses also should be planted in the fall, while warm-season grasses should be planted in the spring.

In northern states, most native wildflowers and grasses are perennials. Although native seeds can be planted in the spring or fall, spring planting is most common. Because of the variable nature of snow melt and spring showers, the exact seeding time is hard to predict. Luckily, warm-season prairie species can be planted any time from mid-spring through June.

Fall seedings are implemented late in the season, after frost, as a dormant planting. The seeds are broadcast or drilled with no expectation of germination until spring. In fact, late germination would only end in winter kill of tender seedlings. During the winter, the seeds will undergo stratification, which breaks dormancy in the majority of northern native seeds.

Ideally, native seeds could be planted following nature's seeding schedule. Since this is logistically impossible for plantings of any size or diversity, an optimal season usually is selected. Knowing more about when wildflowers bloom naturally in your area, and when the rainy season occurs, however, can help you figure out the time periods and conditions necessary for seed formation and germination.

Seeding Methods

Hand-broadcasting is the simplest seeding method, and when done correctly is quite successful. The secret is making sure that the seeds contact the soil directly. Soil contact helps the seed retain moisture, which is necessary for germination, and provides a substrate for seedling growth. For small seeds, mix the seeds with damp sand (four parts sand to one part seeds) for more even distribution. Rake the seeds in or press them into the ground to ensure better seed-to-soil contact.

An adjustable, hand-held mechanical seeder also is effective for many wildflower seeds. For larger areas, agricultural grain drills or cultipacker planters can be used to seed wildflowers.

All plants require water to germinate. If fall rainfall is insufficient, water your planting if possible. Water thoroughly once, then lightly each week until the first frost if it doesn't rain. The soil surface should be kept moist. Frequency is more important than quantity during the first three weeks after planting to ensure germination and seedling survival. During dry southern winters, water a few times in December and January to moisten the soil around the seedlings' roots and help insulate them from cold temperatures. Watering also is an effective cold-and-wet treatment for breaking the dormancy of some spring germinating seeds. If rainfall is light or nonexistent in the spring, water periodically to ensure optimal growth and flowering.

MANAGING YOUR SITE

How you manage your wildflower area and the frequency of management will depend on what look you desire and the conditions and species found on your site. Although certain management techniques such as weeding and burning are standard practices for large-scale restoration plantings, each site requires its own management schedule. In addition, individual species have different management needs and may require a combination of techniques. The amount or degree of maintenance will vary from year to year. Here are some general procedures for maintaining a typical wildflower meadow.

The First Year

Annual species germinate quickly and visually dominate a site during the first year. Although many perennials germinate in the first year, their root growth comprises two to three times the amount of their above-ground vegetation, and they normally do not flower until the second or third year. Native bunch grasses usually do not flower or set seeds the first year either, and depending upon the species, reach heights of only two or three inches by the end of the first growing season. Under favorable environmental conditions, little bluestem, for example, develops a two- to three-inch primary root system before any above-ground shoots appear.

If tall weeds are shading the wildflower seedlings, mow at a height set higher than the seedlings to help suppress annual weeds. A scythe, hand clipper, or weed cutter also will do the job if you don't have a mower, or if the mower blades cannot be set high enough. Because most of the weeds will be annuals, mowing them before they set seeds helps destroy the next season's seed crop. The exact time and height for mowing varies with each site and the species planted. In many cases, hand-weeding or spot applications of an herbicide cannot be avoided, especially if aggressive species or perennial weeds dominate the site.

Annual and biennial wildflowers must be allowed to re-seed to produce a strong stand the next year. Once your meadow wildflowers have bloomed, delay mowing the area until at least half of the late-blooming species have dropped seeds. If you have tall, warm-season native grasses in your meadow, wait until late summer or early fall to mow, to allow them to elongate, flower, and set seed. Never mow mid- to tallgrasses below six inches. Although you can mow the grasses in late fall when they are dormant, you may want to leave them intact until late winter or early spring to provide food and cover for wildlife, and add texture to an otherwise barren winter landscape.

Keep in mind that mowing a meadow of desirable species usually includes leaving the clippings—which may have viable seeds—in place. (To increase the diversity in a moist meadow, however, you must remove any clippings.) Also remove the clippings of any weedy or undesirable species that may have set seeds.

The Second Year

With well-spaced and abundant rainfall, most native bunch grasses will flower and produce seeds by the second year. Some biennial and perennial wildflowers also will begin to bloom. If optimum conditions did not occur the first year, residual seeds from the previous year may germinate.

As your wildflower area fills out, you may choose to re-seed or transplant species to fill in bare spots or to increase the diversity of species, especially the second or third year after seeding.

If annual weeds continue to be a problem, you will need to remove them before they set seeds. The need to weed should taper off as the wildflowers and native grasses become more established.

The Third Year and Beyond

By the third or fourth year, your wildflower area may benefit from a controlled burn, provided enough fuel has accumulated. Fire is a natural process in many ecosystems, and can help reduce woody plants and other invasive species. Burning also stimulates the growth of many native grasses and prairie perennials, and breaks the dormancy of some seeds. Try to determine the fire history of your area before instigating a burn.

Remember that burning is a technique that requires special expertise, and should not be attempted without first consulting experienced experts! Fire is a tool that can enhance or inhibit a species, depending on your goal, and the target species is not the only one that will be affected. When and how you burn depends on what you wish to achieve.

Many areas require permits for burning. Urban areas may have regulations prohibiting prescribed burning. If you are unable or do not wish to burn your meadow, you can continue to control weed invasions and remove excess thatch by mowing or spot-treating with an herbicide.

LITERATURE CITED

Brumback, W. 1988. Collection of Plants From the Wild: One Propagator's View. *Wildflower* 4(2).

Campbell, F. T. 1988. Boycotting the Wild-Plant Trade. *Garden* 12(1).

Scott, J. 1986. Native Plants and the Nursery Trade. *American Horticulturist* 65(6).

Epilobium angustifolium

National Wildflower Research Center Definitions

Cultivar: A cultivar, short for "cultivated variety," is a selection made and maintained by humans through horticultural practices.

Escaped plant: A plant that has escaped from a cultivated garden. Such plants may persist for a short time in natural areas but do not naturalize.

Exotic/Non-native plant: A plant that has been introduced from another area; a plant out of its natural range.

Flora: A compilation of native plants that occur in a particular region or habitat.

Indigenous plants: Wildflowers and other native plants found in a specific geographical area or habitat type; a species indigenous to the piedmont soils of the Southeast, for example.

Native plants: Grasses, sedges, ferns, shrubs, vines, trees, and herbaceous wildflowers that exist in a given region through nonhuman introduction.

Naturalized plants: Plants introduced by humans, either intentionally or accidentally, that have existed successfully in the wild for a sufficient period to have reproduced and survived normal climatic fluctuations.

Propagation: Growing a plant either by seeds (sexually) or by cuttings (vegetatively).

Variety: A subgroup of plants within a species with similar characteristics, such as flower color, resulting from natural genetic variation.

Wildflower: A flowering plant native to a particular region or habitat able to grow and reproduce in the wild without the assistance of humans; normally but not necessarily having attractive showy flowers.

Cornus canadensis

Guidelines for Seed Collecting

Because many native species are not available through commercial sources, collecting seeds from wild populations is often the only way to obtain plants for specific habitats. Strict conservation guidelines, however, must be followed to ensure the least disturbance and the persistence of natural stands.

Areas destined to be developed or destroyed soon provide excellent sites for collecting seeds and plants. However, do not collect on public land; always get permission from the landowner when collecting seeds on private land. Never harvest seeds from rare or endangered species—gather only from plants growing abundantly in any given area so that you do not eradicate an isolated population. At most, take only one-third of the available seeds so enough seeds are left to re-seed and increase the stand. Always identify the plants before collecting any seeds.

HARVESTING THE SEEDS

Collecting seeds at the correct time is crucial to successfully propagating wildland species. Suitable plants are noticed most often when they are flowering, rather than when they are in fruit, so collectors should plan ahead. Early in the season, mark specific plants from which you want to collect seeds. Because dried-up seed stalks are hard to find and almost impossible to identify, mark individual plants with surveyor's flagging, or write down obvious landmarks to help you relocate populations later.

Hand-harvesting wild seeds is necessary when the desired species does not grow in pure stands or the site's topography limits the use of mechanical equipment. Gather fruits from the ground only if they have dropped recently. Reject any fruits or seeds that have lain for awhile on damp ground. Do not collect seeds that have signs of insect or mold damage because they may have started to decay or become infested with insects, and could ruin the rest of your seed harvest if combined with other seeds during storage. Delayed harvesting of species with persistent pods often results in insect-infested seeds.

The size of your planned harvest will dictate the tools and materials that you will need. Basic equipment includes gloves, boots, dropcloths, pruning shears, boxes, baskets, paper, or canvas bags. You can strip many seeds, especially grasses, by hand or shake them onto dropcloths. Screens with large openings often are used to sift seeds or fruits, reducing the amount of material that must dry before threshing. Land managers and restoration ecologists who work on restoration projects in natural areas have invented various seed-harvesting tools, both hand-held (such as the Grin Reaper) and tractor attachments. Commercial seed growers use machines like vacuum strippers, mechanical harvesters, and tractor-drawn seed strippers to gather large quantities of seeds.

Seed Maturation

Proper harvesting requires an understanding of seed ripening, dispersal mechanisms, and the influences of weather on the timing of seed maturation. First, you must be familiar with the approximate flowering and fruiting dates of each species, then be able to recognize the mature fruits or seeds. Experience often is the best teacher in learning to determine whether a seed is mature.

Weather is a key factor in the production of mature seeds. Flowering and fruiting dates, as well as seed quality, vary from year to year and from place to place. An early spring and dry summer, for instance, may cause early seed-set.

After determining the general time in which the fruits or seeds ripen, the next step is to observe the plants carefully. You should begin collecting as soon as the fruits or seeds are mature. Even a few days' delay may be the difference between success and failure in harvesting a good seed crop, especially for those species with seeds that disperse quickly or provide food for wildlife.

Mature seeds are usually dark, firm, and dry. Moist, green seeds probably are immature and will not germinate. If they do germinate, they most likely will produce unhealthy seedlings.

Seed pods or capsules that dehisce (break open and expel seeds) when ripe may mature at staggered intervals, which makes seed collecting difficult. Once the seeds mature, those plants may need to be checked every few days to collect any newly matured seeds. Or you may invert a paper sack or nylon stocking over the seed heads and tie it off with a twist-tie to collect the seeds. Enough light and air will reach the plant to allow it to continue growing, and the sack will hold the seeds as they mature and drop, so you only have to collect seeds once at the end of seed-set.

The flesh of pulpy fruits (such as native plums, cherries, and berries) often becomes soft and changes from green or yellow to red, blue, or purple when ripe. Seeds frequently are mature a week or more before the fleshy fruits change color and drop from the branches. To determine seed maturity, cut open the fruit and see if the seeds are firm, full, and dark.

Seed Cleaning and Preparation

Deciding whether to clean wild-harvested seeds depends on the amount of seeds that you have collected, and the number of individual species in the harvest. If you're harvesting a mixture of species, for instance, the volume of material would be too difficult to separate. If you are collecting seeds for individual species, however, cleaning the seeds will give you a better idea of how many seeds you actually have collected and reduce their storage volume.

Different types of seeds require different cleaning and preparation methods. For plants with seeds in pods, achenes, or other dry coverings, collect the seeds just before or as the pods turn brown and dry, and before they dehisce. A mature pod often will twist and split open as it dries, releasing the seeds. Spread the pods in thin, single layers on canvas dropcloths, screens, or trays raised above the ground to dry. The pods should dry in one to three days, depending on the humidity. Once the seeds have dried, you can extract them from the pods by beating or threshing.

Although not all seeds need to be cleaned before storage, those with pulpy fruits should be cleaned immediately to prevent mold. Remove the pulp of large fruits by hand by rubbing them on a screen, or mashing them with a wooden block, rolling pin, or fruit press. You can clean smaller fruits with a blender, as long as you are careful not to damage the seeds. Blend a small amount of the seeds in a two-to-one ratio with water. Use brief, intermittent agitations at low speed, then strain the mixture to separate the seeds from the pulp.

Though not always necessary, threshing seeds (separating seeds from the rest of the plant) reduces the volume of material to be stored. Discarding the chaff also helps remove seed predators such as insect eggs, mold spores, and other seed-disease vectors. The easiest way to thresh seeds is to rub the collected material against a coarse screen.

(Wear heavy gloves to protect your hands.) A more sophisticated method is to rub the plant material on the screen with one or more paddles covered with rubber matting. Commercial seed growers use mechanical threshers or hammermills, especially on tough fruits that make hand rubbing impossible. Seeds processed in a mill are subjected to a vigorous beating or rolling action between finger-like hammers and a perforated screen, removing excess material when the seeds are forced through the screen.

Seed Storage

The two most critical factors in storing seeds are *constant temperature* and *low humidity*. A temperature of 50 degrees Fahrenheit or less and 50 percent humidity or lower is ideal. In general, fluctuating temperature and humidity harms seeds more than slightly higher *constant* values of each. *The key to storing seeds is finding a cool, dry place that will remain cool and dry throughout the storage period.*

Store the seeds in paper sacks to allow good air circulation and prevent mold. Do not store seeds in plastic bags or other non-breathable containers unless the seeds have been thoroughly air-dried.

Dusting the seeds with a mild insecticide will help prevent insect infestations and kill any pests collected with the seeds. Or you can leave the container open for several days to allow insects to escape, and insert a pest strip to take care of any that remain.

Store the seeds in the refrigerator, not the freezer, until you are ready to plant them. Low temperatures, humidity, and light levels protect seed longevity. If you cannot store the seeds in your refrigerator, store them in a cool, dark, dry place that is protected from insects.

Keep fleshy fruits moist to maintain their viability. If allowed to dry out, they will either germinate prematurely or not at all. Plant the seeds immediately or mix them in a one-to-one ratio of moist sand, sphagnum moss, or a peat-and-perlite mixture, and store them in a cool place. If roots emerge from any seeds during storage, the germinating seeds should be removed and planted immediately.

The viability of stored seeds varies from species to species. Some seeds still may be viable after ten years of storage, while others may not germinate after two years in storage. Ideally, seeds should be planted within one year of collection.

FOR REFERENCE:

Embertson, J. 1979. *Pods: Wildflowers and Weeds in their Final Beauty.* New York: Charles Scribner's Sons.

Emery, D. E. 1988. *Seed Propagation of Native California Plants.* Santa Barbara, California: Santa Barbara Botanic Garden.

Nokes, J. 1986. *How to Grow Native Plants of Texas and the Southwest.* Austin, Texas: Texas Monthly Press.

Phillips, H. 1985. *Growing and Propagating Wild Flowers.* Chapel Hill, N. C.: University of North Carolina Press.

Young, J. and C. Young. 1986. *Collecting, Processing and Germinating Seeds of Wildland Plants.* Portland, Oregon: Timber Press.

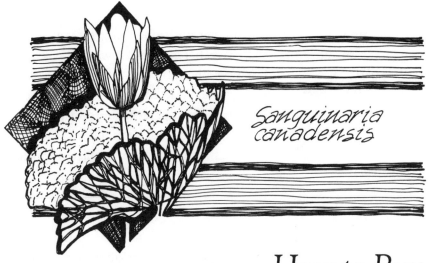

*Sanguinaria
canadensis*

How to Buy
Wildflower Seeds in Bulk

While most seed companies can recommend the amount of seeds to plant for a given area, it is important to remember to ask about *seed quality*. The two most important indicators of seed quality are *germination* and *purity*, and their combined measure, *Pure Live Seed* or *PLS*.

GERMINATION PERCENTAGE

Germination percentage is the proportion of seeds that will germinate under optimum conditions in a seed-testing laboratory. To determine the germination percentage, small samples of seeds from a larger seed lot are tested. The germination percentage on the label may overestimate the success actually seen in the field, but in all cases, the higher the percentage of germination, the better the seeds.

Germination may be low for some flower seeds, especially wild species, because of a hard seed coat, inhibitors, or built-in dormancy mechanisms. Testing seed germination can be a challenge because seeds that do not germinate immediately may still do so later, once their dormancy is broken.

Because the percentage of germination changes over time, depending on how the seeds have been stored, always check the testing date on the label. High temperature and high humidity can have negative effects on seed germination. Many states have seed-labeling laws that require the date of the most recent germination test to appear on the label. Always buy seeds from a reputable source; if you're uncertain, get advice from someone who is familiar with the suppliers.

Purity

Purity indicates the proportion of desired seeds to other components such as noxious weed seeds, crop seeds, and inert matter such as chaff and broken seeds, in a given sample. The purity of a seed lot can be estimated more accurately than the percentage of germination.

PLS or Pure Live Seed

Pure live seed (PLS) takes into consideration both the germination and purity percentages. As a general rule, the higher the PLS, the better the seed quality, although each component is important. Use the following equation to calculate the PLS:

Germination x Purity = PLS

For example:

Seed Lot A:

$$\frac{20\ (\%)\ \text{germination} \times 70\ (\%)\ \text{purity}}{100} = 14\ (\%)\ \text{PLS}$$

Seed Lot B:

$$\frac{70 \text{ (\%) germination} \times 20 \text{ (\%) purity}}{100} = 14 \text{ (\%) PLS}$$

PLS estimates the amount of seeds in a given lot that are good seeds. Both lots have the same PLS, but if higher germination is required, seeds from Lot B would be the best buy. If weed-seed contamination may be a concern, the remaining 80 percent of the purity measure should be checked for noxious weed seeds. If it contains a high proportion of noxious weed seeds, then the seeds from Lot A may be the better buy to minimize future weed control costs.

For seeds with 14 percent PLS, 14 pounds of a 100-pound sack should germinate, given optimum conditions. You can see the value of the PLS percentage more easily when you shop for seeds and compare the PLS with price per pound. Inexpensive seeds with a lower PLS may actually cost more per pound because you need to plant more than higher-priced seeds with a higher PLS. Suppose you want to buy 100 PLS pounds of seeds from one of the two batches of seeds below:

Seed Lot C:

$$\frac{50 \text{ (\%) germ.} \times 70 \text{ (\%) purity}}{100} = 35 \text{ (\%) PLS at \$3/lb.}$$

(.35 seeds/lb. will germinate)

$\frac{100}{.35}$ = 286 pounds of seeds needed to get 100 PLS pounds

286 lbs. $\times$ \$3.00/lb. = \$858.00/100 lbs.
= **\$8.58 per pound of PLS**

Seed Lot D:

$$\frac{70 \text{ (\%) germ.} \times 80 \text{ (\%) purity}}{100} = 56 \text{ (\%) PLS) at \$4/lb.}$$

$$\frac{100}{.56} = 178 \text{ pounds of seeds needed to get 100 PLS pounds}$$

178 lbs. X \$4.00/lb. = \$712.00/100 lbs.
= \$7.12 per pound of PLS

At first glance, the seeds from Lot D appear to be a better buy if you look at just the cost per pound. However, when you account for PLS, Lot D is the better buy of the two seed lots.

Although vegetable, agricultural, and forage crop seeds have been regulated for many years under federal law, flower seed quality has not been regulated or standardized. A few states, however, do enforce quality standards for flower seeds. Seed-testing standards developed by the Association of Official Seed Analysis (AOSA) exist for most agricultural crop species. There are no standard tests yet for most wildflower species, although some development work is in progress.

Shop carefully for wildflower seeds. Start early to determine as many of these factors as possible by obtaining seed catalogs and calling seed producers. Check for the *percentage of germination*, the *date* the germination test was done, and a measure of seed *purity*. You can then calculate the PLS to compare seed quality and price.

Castilleja linariaefolia

How to Propagate Wildflowers from Seed

Successfully propagating wildflowers from seed is a matter of understanding what a seed needs for germination. Seed germination requirements are known for many of the more common wildflower species. However, if you collect seeds from the wild, you may have to determine those requirements on your own, by trial and error.

Observing the natural growing conditions of the plant and the physical characteristics of the seed will provide clues about what the seed needs for germination. Seeds from a shade-loving plant, for example, probably will not germinate if exposed to light. Light would indicate to the seed that it was in the sun, where a mature plant cannot survive. Conversely, excessive darkness could prevent seeds buried too deeply in the soil from germinating, since the seedlings could not survive.

Spring-germinating seeds often have a chilling requirement. This means that the seeds must be cold-stratified (exposed to a prescribed amount of cold) before they will germinate. This mechanism protects the seeds from being fooled into germination by an early temporary warm spell. After a warm winter, seeds requiring cold-stratification may not germinate.

A hard seed may require scarification (nicking or breaking open of the seed coat). Seed scarification occurs naturally through microbial decay, abrasion, or freeze-thaw action, and may take years. Seeds with a hard coat usually have a low germination rate the first year if they are not scarified.

The germination requirement common to all seeds is water. A seed must imbibe (absorb) water before it can respond to other environmental conditions. Once a seed dries out after imbibition, it loses its viability, so you must keep seeds moist throughout all pretreatment phases. Sowing seeds in flats makes it easier to keep them moist.

Due to the variety of germination requirements, it is important to observe seeds carefully to see if they have germinated. If not, you may need to try pretreating the seeds. Sowing seeds in flats is one way to provide the proper environmental conditions necessary for germination, and to monitor the germination rate. After you clean and dry the seeds, place them in a flat containing equal parts of peat, perlite, and vermiculite. Keep tiny seeds on the surface of the medium for maximum exposure to light. Place other seeds at varying depths: some on the surface, some deeper. This will ensure that at least some seeds are at the proper depth and receive the required amount of light. If none of the seeds germinate, try other treatments, such as putting the seeds in a cooler for several weeks, or keeping them in a warm place.

Once the seeds germinate and the seedlings have grown and developed several sets of leaves, it is time to transplant them. Transplant the seedlings directly into a landscape, or into containers such as two- or four-inch pots. Temporarily planting seedlings in pots allows you to observe their growth habits and to control their environment better. It also allows the seedlings to reach a size that may better survive fluctuations in environmental conditions after they are planted into the landscape. In addition, transplanting larger plants also gives you more control of your planting design. You can set plants out while taking size, color, and spacing requirements into account.

Transplanting seedlings into a large-scale wildflower planting may not be economically feasible. Direct seeding usually is most effective; later, you can add plugs to help to fill in gaps. For smaller plantings such as gardens, however, or for planting wild-collected seeds, sowing seeds into flats and then planting the seedlings into the landscape provides more control and better results.

Trillium erectum

Creating a Wildlife Garden

In the past century, accelerated expansion of urban and rural areas has fragmented natural ecosystems and transformed native landscapes into manicured tracts of cultivated, non-native plants, forcing native birds, insects, and small mammals to congregate in disconnected patches of wildflowers and native plants or adjust to altered habitats. Increased interest in lower-maintenance native yards and gardens is leading homeowners to create landscapes that are more compatible with or are an extension of existing ecosystems and their associated wildlife. Such landscapes also provide corridors for animals to move about.

You can make your yard more attractive to wildlife in a variety of ways. Minor changes, such as mowing less often, considerably increase the number of nonhuman visitors to your lot, no matter its size. With the right enticements for wildlife, even tiny yards, rooftop gardens, or porches can become mini-refuges. Hiding places and feeding areas for wildlife can be added without drastically changing the character of your yard. The trick is to create a balance between your needs and those of your "critters." Watching their antics will more than compensate for any inconveniences.

Any wildlife garden must fulfill three basic needs: food, shelter, and water. Diversity is the key to creating habitats that will attract a wider variety of species, offer more choices for forage and shelter, and ensure a constant food supply. Ideally, a garden should offer a mixture of open meadows, woods, and wet areas.

FOOD PREFERENCES

When deciding what to plant, remember that the wildlife your yard attracts will change with the seasons. Migratory species may have different foraging needs than residential (non-migratory) species. Other offerings that attract residential or transient wildlife include pollen, fungi, compost, and sap from native plants.

You also need to consider the developmental needs of wildlife when selecting plants. Larval stages of insects often feed on completely different plants, or parts of plants, from those the adults prefer. Similarly, some species, like butterflies, have highly species-specific needs; they may feed only on one or two types of plants. Monarch butterflies and their larvae, for instance, feed almost exclusively on milkweeds. Nectar-rich wildflowers usually provide more nutritious meals for wildlife than do showy, but often sterile cultivars. Observe insects and animals in natural areas or vacant lots to discover their food preferences.

Butterflies

Relying especially on their keen eyesight, butterflies are attracted to flowers of all shapes, sizes, colors, and fragrances. They usually prefer flowers with yellow, blue, purple, or occasionally red blossoms. Flowers with flat surfaces, clustered florets, or large-lipped petals provide the best conditions for perching, and a greater density of flower heads attracts more butterflies than single flowers. Most butterflies frequent open, sunny areas that are protected from the wind.

A combination of wildflower species and grasses that bloom from early spring through late summer will keep butterflies well-fed throughout the seasons. Members of the composite family such as asters, coreopsis, Joe Pye weed, boneset, goldenrods, sunflowers, and thistles are good nectar sources for butterflies, and later form seedheads that attract goldfinches and other song birds. Small trees such as hawthorns, buckeyes, and sumacs offer nectar sources and shelter.

Moths

Active in the evening or at night, moths depend on a well-developed sense of smell to locate flowers. Like butterflies, moths drink nectar through their long, hollow tongues. Instead of alighting on flowers, however, they hover. Moths visit white, pale yellow, or pink flowers that open at night and emit a strong scent. Moth flowers have deep tubes with open or unfolded margins that allow moths to reach the nectar. Examples of moth flowers include bonesets, evening primroses, yuccas, and cacti.

Some food plants for moth and butterfly larvae include lupine, plantain, pearly everlasting, and dock. Caterpillars also feed on leaves of trees such as birches, aspens, willows, hackberries, and oaks. Milkweeds and thistles provide food for both larval and adult stages.

Bees

Bee-pollinated flowers are typically asymmetrical, and often have a landing platform. Bees especially frequent bright yellow or blue flowers. Some flowers have distinctive patterns invisible to the human eye, called nectar guides, that lead bees to the nectar. Lupines, penstemons, salvias, and orchids are favorites of bees.

Birds

One of the best ways to entice a variety of songbirds is to plant shrubby hedgerows that offer food and shelter. Native honeysuckles, currants, and gooseberries are all good choices. Conifers such as pines and spruces, and deciduous trees such as oaks and maples, provide a smorgasbord of seeds for many birds, while sweet gum is a special favorite of songbirds. Deadwood and duff are good hiding places for insects that feed woodpeckers and other birds. Trees and shrubs with berries provide winter forage for birds and small mammals, while vines and grasses offer both seeds and nesting materials.

Always a favorite of wildlife gardeners, hummingbirds depend on sight rather than smell to locate nectar, and prefer bright red, orange, pink, and occasionally yellow flowers. Hummingbird flowers are tubular, with lots of nectar. Favorite hummingbird flowers include penstemons, salvias, and gilias.

SHELTER SOURCES

When planning shelter for wildlife, try to create a layered effect. Wooded areas should include overlapping canopies of trees, shrubs, and forbs (herbaceous plants). The edges of woods are usually rich with wildlife because they offer both food from open areas and nearby cover to protect them from predators and the elements. Because each species occupies a specific niche or place within a habitat, many different kinds of wildlife often inhabit the same area. For example, different warblers select the top, middle, or lower branches of spruce trees, depending on their species.

When designing shelter areas, including shrubs may be more important than trees because shrubs grow faster and provide nesting sites for many different species. To allow for maximum cover, curb your pruning impulses! Though dense shrubbery, tangled vines, and standing dead trees may be contrary to your image of an orderly yard, they do create ideal sites for nesting and forage.

In a small yard, a single tree or a few vines can provide shelter for nesting wrens or blackbirds, as well as cover for snails and butterflies. And don't overlook leaf litter and other dead materials. Brush piles, hollow logs, and compost piles offer a host of microhabitats for many organisms, including salamanders, earthworms, insect larvae, and other scavengers. Rock walls provide homes for lizards, snakes, and insects. Remember, a yard full of insects will draw lots of birds and other predators!

WATER SOURCES

Water is often the most overlooked and underestimated wildlife need. A significant portion of wildlife activity centers around water, and a water source such as a small pond provides a home for amphibians and aquatic insects, a bathtub for birds, and drinking water for all kinds of creatures. Many insects are aquatic in their larval stages of growth, so they need to be near water. Migrating wildlife also need convenient water sources along their seasonal routes. On the smallest scale, even a birdbath can be a valuable addition to your garden or yard.

MAINTENANCE

Once you allow wildlife into your garden, you must allow nature a bit of freedom in ruling it. As Chris Baines, an innovative British landscaper, notes, "The secret of a successful wildlife garden depends on understanding the way in which your various gardening activities will distort the balance."

Try to minimize disturbance and avoid using chemicals such as herbicides, pesticides, and fungicides, or electric bug zappers, which adversely affect the delicately balanced interactions between organisms and their environment. Allowing your garden more autonomy will leave you plenty of time to observe, enjoy, and learn from your creation.

FOR REFERENCE:

Ernst, R. S. 1987. *The Naturalist's Garden*. Emmaus, Pennsylvania: Rodale Press.

Merilees, B. 1989. *Attracting Backyard Wildlife: A Guide for Nature Lovers*. Stillwater, Minnesota: Voyageur Press.

Peterson, R. T. et al. 1974. *Gardening with Wildlife*. Washington, D.C.: National Wildlife Federation.

Tekulsky, M. 1985. *The Butterfly Garden*. Cambridge, Massachusetts: The Harvard Common Press.

Tufts, C. 1988. *The Backyard Naturalist*. Washington, D.C.: National Wildlife Federation.

Ipomopsis aggregata

Conservation Organizations & Governmental Agencies that Work with Native Plants

Alaska Native Plant Society
P. O. Box 141613
Anchorage, AK 99514
(907)333-8212
A group of amateur and professional botanists using programs and field trips to learn more about Alaskan plants and to educate the public.

Alaska Natural Heritage Program
707 A St., Suite 208
Anchorage, AK 99501
(907)279-4549
A state agency that identifies, lists, manages, and protects rare, threatened, and endangered species.

Alaska Plant Materials Center
USDA, Soil Conservation Service
HC 02 Box 7440
Palmer, AK 99645
(907)745-4469
A state plant materials center supervising projects including the North Latitude Revegetation and Seed Production Project and the North Latitude Vegetable and Landscape Crop Improvement Project.

Nature Conservancy of Alaska, The
601 W. 5th Ave., #550
Anchorage, AK 99501
(907)276-3133
An organization that works for natural land conservation, using acquisition and landowner agreements to maintain the best examples of communities, ecosystems, and endangered species.

Wildflower Garden Club
c/o Verna Pratt
7446 E. 20th
Anchorage, AK 99504
(907)333-8212
A non-profit group of gardeners experimenting with cold climate conditions and growing methods.

Alabama Natural Heritage Program
Folsom Administration Building
64 N. Union St., Rm. 752
Montgomery, AL 36130
(205)242-3007
A state agency that identifies, lists, manages, and protects Alabama's rare, threatened, and endangered species.

Alabama Wildflower Society, The
c/o George Wood, editor
11120 Ben Clements Rd.
Northport, AL 35476
(205)339-2511
A wildflower society devoted to the native plants of Alabama.

Birmingham Botanical Gardens
2612 Lane Park Rd.
Birmingham, AL 35223
(205)879-1227
A municipally owned and operated garden supported by public donations and volunteers who develop and maintain numerous gardens and collections.

Huntsville/Madison County Botanical Garden
4747 Bob Wallace Ave.
Huntsville, AL 35805
A 35-acre landscaped tract featuring distinctive gardens and offering public tours, educational field trips, workshops, and free lectures.

Nature Conservancy, The
Alabama Field Office
806-D 29th St. S
Birmingham, AL 35205
(205)836-9002
An organization that works for natural land conservation, using acquisition and landowner agreements to maintain the best examples of communities, ecosystems, and endangered species.

Troy State University Arboretum
236 Adams Center
Troy, AL 36082
(205)566-3000
A 75-acre arboretum and nature center focusing on education and rare species preservation.

University of Alabama Arboretum
P. O. Box 870344
Tuscaloosa, AL 35487-0344
(205)348-5960
A non-profit arboretum affiliated with the University of Alabama.

Arkansas Native Plant Society
Attn: Bruce Ewing
Rt. 2 Box 256BB
Mena, AR 71953
(501)394-4666
A non-profit organization promoting the preservation, conservation, and study of Arkansas' native vegetation.

Arkansas Natural Heritage Commission
Suite 200, The Heritage Center
225 E. Markham
Little Rock, AR 72201
(501)371-1706
A state agency that identifies, lists, manages, and protects rare, threatened, and endangered species.

Booneville Plant Materials Center
USDA, Soil Conservation Service
Rt. 2 Box 144B
Booneville, AR 72927
(501)675-5182
A plant materials center that finds and evaluates plants to solve specific conservation problems, then develops foundation seed sources for commercial seed growers.

Nature Conservancy, The
Arkansas Field Office
300 Spring Bldg., Suite 717
Little Rock, AR 72201
(501)372-2750
An organization that works for natural land conservation, using acquisition and landowner agreements to maintain the best examples of communities, ecosystems, and endangered species.

Arboretum at Flagstaff, The
P. O. Box 670
South Woody Mountain Road
Flagstaff, AZ 86002
(602)774-1441
An arboretum with a plant collection and a horticultural research program that studies dry, high-elevation plant communities in the western United States.

Arizona Heritage Progam/Nongame Branch
Arizona Game and Fish Department
2221 W. Greenway Rd.
Phoenix, AZ 85023
(602)942-3000
A state agency that identifies, lists, manages, and protects rare, threatened, and endangered species.

Arizona Native Plant Society
P. O. Box 41206
Sun Station
Tucson, AZ 85704
A society working to broaden knowledge of Arizona native flora and promote their use and conservation.

Arizona-Sonora Desert Museum
2021 N. Kinney Rd.
Tucson, AZ 85743
(602)883-1380
A museum that exhibits and interprets the flora, fauna, and geology of the Sonoran Desert region with an ecological focus.

Boyce Thompson Southwestern Arboretum
P. O. Box AB
Superior, AZ 85273
(602)689-2723
An arboretum dedicated to collecting plants from arid regions of the world.

Desert Botanical Garden
1201 N. Galvin Parkway
Phoenix, AZ 85008
(602)941-1225
A research collection concentrating on floristics of deserts of the world, especially in the southwestern United States.

Nature Conservancy, The
Arizona Field Office
300 E. University, Suite 230
Tucson, AZ 85705
(602)622-3861
An organization that works for natural land conservation, using acquisition and landowner agreements to maintain the best examples of communities, ecosystems, and endangered species.

Nature Conservancy, The
Phoenix Office
2255 N. 44th St., #100
Phoenix, AZ 85008
(602)220-0490
An organization that works for natural land conservation, using acquisition and landowner agreements to maintain the best examples of communities, ecosystems, and endangered species.

Navajo Natural Heritage Program
Navajo Fish and Wildlife
P. O. Box O
Window Rock, AZ 86515
(602)871-6472
An agency that inventories the elements of natural diversity on the Navajo Nation: plants, animals, and communities.

Tohono Chul Park, Inc.
7366 N. Paseo del Norte
Tucson, AZ 85704
(602)742-6455
A 36-acre non-profit preserve promoting the conservation of arid regions, providing an opportunity to learn about and experience the desert, and encouraging water conservation and the use of native plants. Facilities include demonstration and ethnobotanical gardens, nature trails, greenhouse, and exhibit house.

Tucson Botanical Gardens
2150 N. Alvernon Way
Tucson, AZ 85712
(602)326-9255
A 5-acre botanical garden in the geographic center of Tucson devoted to education and the display of local horticultural possibilities.

Tucson Plant Materials Center
USDA, Soil Conservation Service
3241 N. Romero Rd.
Tucson, AZ 85705
(602)670-6491
A plant materials center that finds and evaluates plants to solve specific conservation problems, then develops foundation seed sources for commercial seed growers.

American Herbalists Guild
P. O. Box 1683
Soquel, CA 95073
(408)438-1700, ext. 273
An organization working to improve competence and skill in all areas of medical herbalism.

California Department of Fish and Game
Endangered Plant Program
1416 9th St., 12th Floor
Sacramento, CA 95814
(916)322-2493
A state agency that identifies, lists, manages, and protects California's rare, threatened, and endangered plants.

California Native Plant Society
909 12th St., Suite 116
Sacramento, CA 95814
(916)447-2677
A society dedicated to the preservation of California's native flora for future generations.

California Natural Heritage Division
Department of Fish and Game
1416 9th St., 12th Floor
Sacramento, CA 95814
(916)322-2493
A state agency that identifies, lists, manages, and protects rare, threatened, and endangered species.

Descanso Gardens Guild, Inc.
1418 Descanso Dr.
La Canada, CA 91011
(818)790-3261
The guild supports all functions of Descanso Gardens, a 60-acre garden with formal and natural landscapes.

Environmental Study Area
De Anza College
21250 Stevens Creek Blvd.
Cupertino, CA 95014
(408)864-8657
A study area containing 12 native California plant communities with more than 270 species.

Julian Woman's Club
P. O. Box 393
Julian, CA 92036
(619)765-1876
The club, a member of the General Federation of Women's Clubs, organizes an annual wildflower and native plant show.

Living Desert, The
47900 Portola Ave.
Palm Desert, CA 92260
(619)346-5694
A 1,200-acre preserve and botanical garden focusing on the conservation of world deserts.

Lockeford Plant Materials Center
USDA, Soil Conservation Service
P. O. Box 68
Lockeford, CA 95237
(209)727-5319
A plant materials center that finds and evaluates plants to solve specific conservation problems, then develops foundation seed sources for commercial seed growers.

Lummis Garden Project
Historical Society of Southern California
200 E. Ave. 43
Los Angeles, CA 90031
(213)222-0546
A non-profit, membership-based historical society headquartered in the turn-of-the-century Lummis Home. In 1985, the nearly two-acre garden surrounding the home was redesigned as a model residential water-conserving garden.

Mendocino Coast Botanical Gardens
P. O. Box 1143
Fort Bragg, CA 95437-1143
(707)964-4352
A 47-acre public garden with a coastal pine forest and ocean bluffs containing plant collections that thrive in a Mediterranean climate.

Nature Conservancy, The
California Field Office
785 Market St., 3rd Floor
San Francisco, CA 94103
(415)777-0487
An organization that works for natural land conservation, using acquisition and landowner agreements to maintain the best examples of communities, ecosystems, and endangered species.

Rancho Santa Ana Botanic Garden
1500 N. College Ave.
Claremont, CA 91711
(714)625-8767
A botanic garden that emphasizes research, education, and conservation, especially concerning the flora of California, Mexico, and the Mediterranean countries.

San Joaquin Delta College
Natural Science Department
5151 Pacific Ave.
Stockton, CA 95207
A community college that maintains a nature trail at a field laboratory in the mountains.

Santa Barbara Botanic Garden
1212 Mission Canyon Rd.
Santa Barbara, CA 93105
(805)682-4726
A garden dedicated to the study, display, and preservation of California's native flora, and offering an extensive public education program.

Southern California Botanists
Biology Department
California State University
Fullerton, CA 92634
(714)773-3614
An organization devoted to the study, preservation, and conservation of native plants and plant communities of Southern California.

Strybing Arboretum and Botanical Gardens
Golden Gate Park
9th Avenue at Lincoln Way
San Francisco, CA 94122
(415)753-7089
An arboretum specializing in plant collections from the five Mediterranean climates of the world, and including special collections of magnolias, rhododendrons, and succulent plants, as well as Japanese gardens and a fragrance garden for the visually challenged.

The Institute for the Study of Natural Systems
P. O. Box 637
Mill Valley, CA 94942
(415)383-5064
An institute focusing on environmental education and restoration with a cross-cultural emphasis.

Theodore Payne Foundation
10459 Tuxford St.
Sun Valley, CA 91352
(818)768-1802
A non-profit organization working to preserve California native plants, and operating a nursery carrying more than 600 species of native plants and wildflower seed varieties.

University of California Botanical Garden
Centennial Drive
Berkeley, CA 94720
(415)642-3343
A university botanical garden with one of the largest collections of living plants in North America, and more than 10,000 species from around the world.

American Penstemon Society
1569 S. Holland Court
Lakewood, CO 80226
(303)986-8096
A society dedicated to the advancement of knowledge about penstemons, their introduction to cultivation, and the development of new and improved cultivars.

Betty Ford Alpine Gardens
183 Gore Creek Dr. (office only)
(gardens located in Gerald Ford Park)
Vail, CO 81657
(303)476-0103
A garden that collects and displays herbaceous plants, trees, and shrubs native primarily to the Rocky Mountains and educates the public about the wide variety of plant material that can be grown in mountain communities.

Colorado Native Plant Society
P. O. Box 200
Fort Collins, CO 80522
A non-profit organization dedicated to preservation of the Colorado flora and education.

Colorado Natural Areas Program
Division of Parks and Outdoor Recreation
1313 Sherman St., Room 618
Denver, CO 80203
(303)866-2597
A state agency that identifies, lists, manages, and protects rare, threatened, and endangered species.

Denver Botanic Garden
909 York St.
Denver, CO 80206-3799
(303)331-4000
A display garden with a research emphasis on regional horticulture.

Meeker Plant Materials Center
USDA, Soil Conservation Service
P. O. Box 448
Meeker, CO 81641
(303)878-5003
One of the network of plant materials centers located throughout the United States.

Nature Conservancy, The
Colorado Field Office
1244 Pine S.
Boulder, CO 80302
(303)444-2950
An organization that works for natural land conservation, using acquisition and landowner agreements to maintain the best examples of communities, ecosystems, and endangered species.

Connecticut Botanical Society, Inc.
Osborn Memorial Laboratory (Herbarium)
167 Prospect St.
New Haven, CT 06511
(203)388-6148
A society organized to obtain a thorough knowledge of the wild plants of Connecticut.

Connecticut College Arboretum
P. O. Box 5511, Connecticut College
270 Mohegan Ave.
New London, CT 06320
(203)447-1911
An arboretum with a 20-acre native tree and shrub collection and 400+ acres of natural areas open to the public with no admission charge.

Connecticut Natural Diversity Database
State Office Building, Room 553
165 Capitol Ave.
Hartford, CT 06106
(203)566-3540
A state agency that identifies, lists, manages, and protects rare, threatened, and endangered species.

Fairfield Historical Society
636 Old Post Rd.
Fairfield, CT 06430
(203)259-1598
A society that operates Ogden House, a 1750 farm site that includes a one-acre wildflower area of native plants.

Flanders Nature Center, Inc.
P. O. Box 702
Woodbury, CT 06798
(203)263-3711
A teaching nature center, community resource center, and land trust managing more than 1,200 acres.

National Environmental Education Center
613 Riversville Rd.
Greenwich, CT 06831
(203)869-5272
An education center that is part of the National Aubudon Society, a national conservation organization.

Nature Conservancy, The
Connecticut Field Office
55 High St.
Middletown, CT 06457
(203)344-0716
An organization that works for natural land conservation, using acquisition and landowner agreements to maintain the best examples of communities, ecosystems, and endangered species.

New Canaan Nature Center
144 Oenoke Ridge
New Canaan, CT 06840
(203)966-9577
A private, non-profit education organization dedicated to increasing understanding and concern for the natural world.

Committee for the National Institutes for the Environment
730 Eleventh St. NW
Washington, DC 20001-4521
(202)628-4303
A group of scientists, environmentalists, and concerned citizens working to increase support for environmental research, training, and public policy. The group supports creating the National Institutes for the Environment, a federal entity that would fund mission-oriented, multi-disciplinary research on a variety of environmental problems.

Natural Resources Defense Council
1350 New York Ave. NW
Washington, DC 20005
(202)783-7800
An environmental organization that promotes conservation and wise use of the natural environment.

U.S. National Arboretum, U.S. Department of Agriculture
3501 New York Ave. NE
Washington, DC 20002
(202)475-4855
A research and educational facility dedicated to the improvement and display of landscape plants, primarily trees and shrubs.

❖————————————————————————————————

Delaware Federation of Garden Clubs
Attn: Olivia Kirby Thomas
2016 Naamens Rd., F-14
Wilmington, DE 19810
(302)475-7626
A federated garden club teaching and working in all phases of gardening, flower arranging, community projects, civic work, and environmental and waste management. The federation works with the Delaware Dept. of Transportation on improving and beautifying roads using wildflowers.

Delaware Natural Heritage Program
Division of Parks and Recreation
89 Kings Highway
Dover, DE 19903
(302)739-5285
A state agency that identifies, lists, manages, and protects rare, threatened, and endangered species.

Delaware Nature Society
P. O. Box 700
Hockessin, DE 19707
(302)239-2334
A 6,000-member non-profit society working for a better understanding of the environment and our relationship with it. The society, dedicated to the preservation of representative natural areas and to environmental education at all levels, has facilities in Hockessin and Milford.

Mt. Cuba Center for the Study of Piedmont Flora
P. O. Box 3570
Greenville, DE 19807
(302)239-4244
A private garden being developed for the public to further the appreciation, conservation, and use of native Piedmont plants.

Nature Conservancy, The
Delaware Field Office
P. O. Box 1324
Dover, DE 19903-1324
(302)674-3550
An organization that works for natural land conservation, using acquisition and landowner agreements to maintain the best examples of communities, ecosystems, and endangered species.

Brooksville Plant Materials Center
USDA, Soil Conservation Service
14119 Broad St.
Brooksville, FL 34601
(904)754-0303
A plant materials center that finds and evaluates plants to solve specific conservation problems, then develops foundation seed sources for commercial seed growers.

Florida Defenders of the Environment
2606 N.W. 6th St.
Gainesville, FL 32609
(904)372-6965
A group that promotes the conservation, restoration, and wise use of Florida's natural resources by providing objective information and analysis developed by a statewide network of volunteer specialists.

Florida Department of Agriculture and Consumer Services
2043 San Marino S
Clearwater, FL 34623
(813)446-6994
An agency that protects Florida's native and commercially grown plants from harmful pests and diseases.

Florida Federation of Garden Clubs, Inc.
P. O. Box 1604
1400 S. Denning Dr.
Winter Park, FL 32790
(407)647-7016
A non-profit garden club that educates its members and the public in the fields of gardening, horticulture, botany, landscape design, conservation of natural resources, civic beautification, public sanitation, and nature studies. The federation also helps with roadside beautification projects.

Florida Native Plant Society
P. O. Box 680008
Orlando, FL 32868
(407)299-1472
The society supports the preservation, conservation, and restoration of Florida's native plants and native plant communities.

Florida Natural Areas Inventory
1018 Thomasville Rd., Suite 200-C
Tallahassee, FL 32303
(904)224-8207
A statewide database on the occurrence and management of rare or endangered species, natural communities, and managed areas.

Nature Conservancy, The
Florida Field Office
2699 Lee Rd., Suite 500
Winter Park, FL 32789
(407)628-5887
An organization that works for natural land conservation, using acquisition and landowner agreements to maintain the best examples of communities, ecosystems, and endangered species.

Nature Conservancy, The
Florida Keys Protection Project
P. O. Box 4958
Key West, FL 33041
(305)296-3880
An organization that works for natural land conservation, using acquisition and landowner agreements to maintain the best examples of communities, ecosystems, and endangered species.

Sanibel Captiva Conservation Foundation Native Plant Nursery
P. O. Box 839
Sanibel, FL 33957
(813)472-1932
A non-profit conservation center that buys land and preserves wildlife habitat.

Americus Plant Materials Center
USDA, Soil Conservation Service
Rt. 6 Box 417
Americus, GA 31709
(912)924-2286
A plant materials center that finds and evaluates plants to solve specific conservation problems, then develops foundation seed sources for commercial seed growers.

Atlanta Botanical Garden
P. O. Box 77246
1345 Piedmont Rd.
Atlanta, GA 30357
(404)876-5859
A botanical garden whose mission is to educate the public and develop and maintain plant collections for display and research.

Atlanta Historical Society
3101 Andrews Drive NW
Atlanta, GA 30305
(404)261-1837
A history museum and gardens (native plant and period gardens) that tell the history of Atlanta and environs.

Callaway Gardens
Ida Cason Callaway Foundation
U.S. Highway 27
Pine Mountain, GA 31822-2000
(404)663-5020
A horticultural display garden educates and interprets the natural world for visitors.

Fernbank Science Center
156 Heaton Park Dr.
Atlanta, GA 30307
(404)378-4311
A comprehensive science education organization operated by the Dekalb County School System. Facilities include a planetarium, observatory, exhibit hall with museum displays, greenhouses and garden areas, laboratories, classrooms, and a 65-acre forest with nature trails.

Freshwater Wetlands and Heritage Inventory
Georgia Department of Natural Resources
Rt. 2 Box 119 D
Social Circle, GA 30279
(404)557-2514
The program uses The Nature Conservancy's heritage methodology to track rare native plants in Georgia. Other concerns are environmental review, plant rescue, and population biology research.

Garden Club of Georgia, Inc., The
325 S. Lumpkin St.
Athens, GA 30602
A state garden club affiliated with the National Council of State Garden Clubs.

Georgia Experiment Station
Department of Horticulture
1109 Experiment St.
Griffin, GA 30223
(404)228-7243
An experiment station that conducts research involving establishment and management of wildflowers for roadside beautification and meadows for public and private lands.

Nature Conservancy, The
Georgia Field Office
1401 Peachtree St. NE, #136
Atlanta, GA 30309
(404)263-9225
An organization that works for natural land conservation, using acquisition and landowner agreements to maintain the best examples of communities, ecosystems, and endangered species.

State Botanical Garden of Georgia, The
The University of Georgia
2450 S. Milledge Ave.
Athens, GA 30605
(404)542-1244
A public, non-profit educational organization under the auspices of the University of Georgia.

Harold L. Lyon Arboretum
University of Hawaii
3860 Manoa Rd.
Honolulu, HI 96822
(808)988-3177
An organized research unit of the University of Hawaii established to facilitate, promote, and execute research, instruction, and public service about tropical plants.

Hawaii Heritage Program
1116 Smith St., #201
Honolulu, HI 96817
(808)537-4508
A state agency that identifies, lists, manages, and protects rare, threatened, and endangered species.

Hawaii Plant Conservation Center
National Tropical Botanical Garden
P. O. Box 340
Lawai, HI 96765
(808)332-7324, ext. 24
A resource center dedicated to the collection, propagation, study, and distribution of native Hawaiian plants.

Hawaii Plant Materials Center
USDA, Soil Conservation Service
P. O. Box 236
Hoolehua, HI 96729
(808)567-6378
A center that tests and releases plant materials for soil and water conservation.

Honolulu Botanical Gardens
50 N. Vineyard Blvd.
Honolulu, HI 96817
(808)533-3406
A garden encompassing approximately 700 acres including Foster/ Lili'uokalani, Ho'omaluhia, Koko Crater, and Wahiawa Botanical Gardens, among others.

National Tropical Botanical Garden
P. O. Box 340
Lawai, HI 96765
(808)332-7324
A private botanical garden chartered by the United States Congress to create a national resource in tropical botany.

Nature Conservancy, The
Hawaii Field Office
1116 Smith St., Suite 201
Honolulu, HI 96817
(808)537-4508
An organization that works for natural land conservation, using acquisition and landowner agreements to maintain the best examples of communities, ecosystems, and endangered species.

Bickelhaupt Arboretum
340 S. 14th St.
Clinton, IA 52732
(319)242-4771
A privately financed, public arboretum featuring native prairie land.

Federated Garden Clubs of Iowa
Rt. 1 Box 148
Spencer, IA 51301
(712)262-3548
A member of the National Council of State Garden Clubs and coordinator of the state's annual Operation Wildflower workshop. Operation Wildflower is dedicated to beautification and to public education about native wildflowers and grasses.

Indian Creek Nature Center
6665 Otis Rd. SE
Cedar Rapids, IA 52403
(319)362-0664
Located five miles from downtown Cedar Rapids, the 140-acre preserve includes native prairie, oak/hickory savanna, meadow, and riparian woodlands. The center provides environmental education, public programming, and technical advice.

Iowa Natural Areas Inventory
Department of Natural Resources
Wallace State Office Building
Des Moines, IA 50319-0034
(515)281-8524
A state agency that inventories private and public natural areas for rare species of plants and animals including good examples of plant communities.

Iowa Prairie Network
5266 Lakeview Dr.
Clear Lake, IA 50428
(515)357-6752; Hotline: (402)572-3080
A network to improve communication among those concerned about Iowa's natural heritage. Seven local regions provide a communication framework and hands-on experience through stewardship activities, field trips, identification of new sites, and management of natural areas in the regions.

Nature Conservancy, The
Iowa Field Office
431 E. Locust St., Suite 200
Des Moines, IA 50309
(515)244-5044
An organization that works for natural land conservation, using acquisition and landowner agreements to maintain the best examples of communities, ecosystems, and endangered species.

Project GREEN
Civic Center
Iowa City, IA 52240
(319)351-5625
A citizen-action group established in 1967 to preserve and improve the natural and human-made environment and to encourage high standards of design and community appearance.

Aberdeen Plant Materials Center
USDA, Soil Conservation Service
P. O. Box AA
Aberdeen, ID 83210
(208)397-4181
A plant materials center that finds and evaluates plants to solve specific conservation problems, then develops foundation seed sources for commercial seed growers.

Idaho Native Plant Society
P. O. Box 9451
Boise, ID 83707
(208)334-1457
A non-profit membership organization with four chapters that promote interest in Idaho's native flora and collect and disseminate information about the state's native plants.

Idaho Natural Heritage Program
Idaho Department of Fish and Game
600 S. Walnut St., Box 25
Boise, ID 83707
(208)334-3402
A state agency that collects, stores, and distributes data on the location and status of rare plant and animal populations and ecosystems in Idaho as part of the natural heritage network.

Nature Conservancy, The
Idaho Field Office
P. O. Box 165
Sun Valley, ID 83353
(208)726-3007
An organization that works for natural land conservation, using acquisition and landowner agreements to maintain the best examples of communities, ecosystems, and endangered species.

Chicago Botanic Garden
P. O. Box 400
Glencoe, IL 60022
(312)835-5440
A 300-acre garden featuring formal gardens, native landscape restoration, and tree collections in a park-like setting. It is dedicated to education, conservation, and research.

Citizens for Conservation
P. O. Box 435
Barrington, IL 60011
(708)382-7283
A volunteer organization active in natural areas acquisition and management, wildlife preservation, prairie and savanna restorations, and environmental education.

Evanston Environmental Association
2024 McCormick
Evanston, IL 60201
(708)864-5181
A center promoting programs and services that focus on environmental education.

Friends of the Indian Boundary Prairies
P. O. Box 394
Markham, IL 60426
(815)469-3937
A group, associated with The Nature Conservancy's Volunteer Stewardship Network, which helps manage the Ginsburg, Paintbrush, Sundrop, and Dropseed prairies.

Glacial Park
6512 Harts Rd.
Ringwood, IL 60072
(815)628-4431
A natural area with an on-site nursery for prairie and savanna species, with a technician on duty from April to October.

Grand Prairie Friends of Illinois
P. O. Box 36
Urbana, IL 61801
A non-profit conservation organization dedicated to the preservation and management of the tallgrass prairie, particularly in east-central Illinois.

Green Earth, Inc.
P. O. Box 441
Carbondale, IL 62903
(618)457-4780
A non-profit organization working to preserve natural areas in the Carbondale area and offering educational programs. Preserves are open to the public all year.

Illinois Dunesland Preservation Society
410 Deer Path Dr.
Winthrop Harbor, IL 60096
(708)746-1090
A society supporting the Illinois Dunes State Park.

Illinois Native Plant Society
Forest Glen Preserve
Rt. 1 Box 495A
Westville, IL 61883
(217)662-2142
A group with six chapters promoting the preservation, understanding, and appreciation of the native flora and natural communities of Illinois.

Illinois Natural Heritage Division
Department of Conservation
524 S. 2nd St.
Springfield, IL 62706
(217)785-8774
A state agency that identifies, lists, manages, and protects rare, threatened, and endangered species.

Illinois Prairie Path, The
P. O. Box 1086
Wheaton, IL 60187
(708)665-5310
A non-profit corporation that assists government agencies in maintaining a multi-purpose trail and its associated natural areas including prairie remnants. The trail, The Illinois Prairie Path, is located mostly on an abandoned railroad right-of-way running through the western suburbs of Chicago.

Land Preservation, Inc.
5 S 747 Rt. 47
Sugar Grove, IL 60554
(708)466-4922
A non-profit organization that raises funds for the preservation of natural lands.

Lee County Natural Areas Guardians
Lee County S&WCD
Amboy, IL 61310
(815)857-3623
A volunteer group interested in locating, managing, and promoting natural areas.

Lincoln Memorial Garden and Nature Center
2301 E. Lake Shore Dr.
Springfield, IL 62707
(217)529-1111
A garden designed by Jens Jensen (a landscape architect who pioneered the use of native plants in the designed landscape) and composed of plants native to the states where Abraham Lincoln lived—Kentucky, Indiana, and Illinois.

McHenry County Defenders' Wildflower Preservation and Propagation Committee
c/o Lou Emmons
7805 Tryon Grove Rd.
Richmond, IL 60071
(815)678-4383
A committee organized to stimulate interest in wildflowers and inform the people of McHenry County of the need to protect them. Volunteers seek to propagate and reintroduce into natural areas plants that records show once grew there.

McHenry County Natural Area Volunteers
329 Carl Sands Dr.
Cary, IL 60013
(708)516-3614
An organization associated with The Nature Conservancy's Volunteer Stewardship Network, which helps manage the natural areas of McHenry County

Morton Arboretum, The
Route 53
Lisle, IL 60532
(708)968-0074
A 1,500-acre outdoor museum of woody plants with displays of trees, shrubs, and vines from around the north-temperate world.

Natural Areas Association
320 S. Third St.
Rockford, IL 61104-1098
(815)964-6666
A non-profit organization that works to inform, unite, and support persons engaging in identifying, protecting, managing, and studying natural areas and biological diversity.

Natural Land Institute
320 S. Third St.
Rockford, IL 61104-1098
(815)964-6666
A group organized in 1958 to preserve ecologically significant areas and the native plants and animals that inhabit them for their educational, scientific, historical, and aesthetic values.

Nature Conservancy, The
Illinois Field Office
79 W. Monroe St., Suite 900
Chicago, IL 60603
(312)346-8166
An organization that works for natural land conservation, using acquisition and landowner agreements to maintain the best examples of communities, ecosystems, and endangered species.

North Branch Prairie Project
P. O. Box 74
Northbrook, IL 60065
(312)431-0158
A volunteer group that cooperates with the Sierra Club-Chicago, Chicago Audubon Society, and The Nature Conservancy to manage prairie remnants along the north branch of the Chicago River for the Cook County Forest Preserve District.

Save the Prairie Society
10327 Elizabeth St.
Westchester, IL 60154
(708)865-8736
A organization devoted to preserving and managing the 85-acre Wolf Road Prairie as a dedicated Illinois Nature Preserve and a nominated National Natural Landmark.

The Nature Institute
c/o Sarah F. Perkins, President
2888 Adams Parkway
Alton, IL 62002
(618)463-0766
A non-profit organization that promotes nature education for all ages and the preservation and management of natural ecosystems.

West Chicago Prairie Stewardship Group
c/o Mel Hoff
29 W. 300 Iroquois Court
Warrenville, IL 60555
(708)393-4715
A volunteer organization working with the DuPage County Forest Preserve District to aid in the management and preservation of the 300-acre West Chicago Prairie and a member of the Volunteer Network sponsored by The Nature Conservancy.

Wetland Resources Center
Max McGraw Wildlife Foundation
P. O. Box 9
Dundee, IL 60118
(708)741-8000
A not-for-profit private foundation dedicated to wildlife and fisheries management and conservation, and conservation education.

Whiteside County Natural Area Guardians
USDA Bldg.
Rt. 1, 16255 Liberty Street
Morrison, IL 61270
(815)772-3811
An active subcommittee of the Soil and Water Conservation District dedicated to the preservation, restoration, and management of natural areas.

ACRES, Inc.
P. O. Box 140
1802 Chapman Rd.
Huntertown, IN 46748
(219)637-6264
An organization with 26 nature preserves in northeast Indiana with the prime purpose of saving natural habitat and threatened species. The group conducts educational programs in the field and indoors.

Indiana Heritage Program
Division of Nature Preserves
Room 605B, State Office Building
Indianapolis, IN 46204
(317)232-4052
A state agency that identifies, inventories, and protects Indiana's native flora, fauna, and natural communities.

Nature Conservancy, The
Indiana Field Office
1330 W. 38th St.
Indianapolis, IN 46208
(317)923-7547
An organization that works for natural land conservation, using acquisition and landowner agreements to maintain the best examples of communities, ecosystems, and endangered species.

Dyck Arboretum of the Plains
Hesston College
P. O. Box 3000
Hesston, KS 67062
(316)327-8127
A 30-acre arboretum featuring plants native to Kansas to foster an appreciation of the state's natural beauty.

Kansas Natural Heritage Inventory
Kansas Biological Survey
2041 Constant Ave.
Lawrence, KS 66047-2906
(913)864-3453
A computer-assisted inventory of biological diversity in Kansas that maintains data on the status, location, and distribution of rare plants and animals and outstanding examples of natural communities in the state.

Kansas Wildflower Society
Mulvane Art Center
Washburn University
Topeka, KS 66621
(913)267-4044
A society organized for the enjoyment, study, and preservation of native plants in Kansas.

Konza Prairie Research Natural Area
Division of Biology, Kansas State University
Manhattan, KS 66506-4091
(913)532-6620
An 8,600-acre tract of native tallgrass prairie owned by The Nature Conservancy, and leased to Kansas State University for preservation, education, and long-term ecological research.

Manhattan Plant Materials Center
USDA, Soil Conservation Service
3800 S. 20th St.
Manhattan, KS 66502
(913)539-8761
A plant materials center that finds and evaluates plants to solve specific conservation problems, then develops foundation seed sources for commercial seed growers.

Nature Conservancy, The
Kansas Field Office
3601 W. 29th St., Suite 112-B
Topeka, KS 66614
(913)272-5115
An organization that works for natural land conservation, using acquisition and landowner agreements to maintain the best examples of communities, ecosystems, and endangered species.

Division of Natural Areas
Eastern Kentucky University
McCreary Building 224
Richmond, KY 40475
(606)622-1476
An agency that manages university-owned natural areas and works closely with federal and state agencies on nature preserve matters, environmental assessment analysis, and monitoring.

I.W. Bernheim Foundation
Bernheim Forest and Arboretum
Highway 245
Clermont, KY 40110
(502)543-2451
A 10,000-acre arboretum and forest located 20 miles south of Louisville.

Kentucky Heritage Program
Kentucky Nature Preserves Commission
407 Broadway
Frankfort, KY 40601
(502)564-2886
An agency that inventories and protects rare species and natural communities in the state of Kentucky.

Kentucky Native Plant Society
Department of Biological Sciences
Eastern Kentucky University
Richmond, KY 40475
(606)622-6257
An organization to promote conservation, education, research, and information exchange about Kentucky's native vegetation.

Nature Conservancy, The
Kentucky Chapter
642 W. Main St.
Lexington, KY 40508-2018
(606)259-9655
An organization that works for natural land conservation, using acquisition and landowner agreements to maintain the best examples of communities, ecosystems, and endangered species.

Quicksand Plant Materials Center
USDA, Soil Conservation Service
University Drive
Quicksand, KY 41363-9999
(606)666-5069
A government agency that assembles, tests, and releases plant materials for conservation use.

Lafayette Natural History Museum
637 Girard Park Dr.
Lafayette, LA 70503
(318)261-8350
A city-owned facility composed of a museum, planetarium, and nature station dedicated to the enhancement of environmental conservation and education.

Louisiana Natural Heritage Program
Department of Wildlife and Fisheries
P. O. Box 98000
Baton Rouge, LA 70898-9000
(504)765-2821
A state endangered species program that monitors rare plants, animals, and habitats.

Louisiana Nature and Science Center
P. O. Box 870610
New Orleans, LA 70187-0610
(504)246-5672
An environmental education organization located in an 86-acre suburban woodland.

Louisiana Plant Materials Center
USDA, Soil Conservation Service
P. O. Box 629
Thibodaux, LA 70302
(504)447-3871
A plant materials center that finds and evaluates plants to solve specific conservation problems, then develops foundation seed sources for commercial seed growers.

Louisiana Project Wildflower
c/o Lafayette Natural History Museum
637 Girard Park Dr.
Lafayette, LA 70503
(318)261-8350
An organization dedicated to the preservation, conservation, and propagation of Louisiana's native plant community with particular emphasis on roadside populations.

Nature Conservancy, The
Louisiana Field Office
P. O. Box 4125
Baton Rouge, LA 70821
(504)338-1040
An organization that works for natural land conservation, using acquisition and landowner agreements to maintain the best examples of communities, ecosystems, and endangered species.

American Wildflower Society
Bluet Meadow
17 Le Clair Terrace
Chicopee, MA 01013
An organization dedicated to promoting greater appreciation and awareness of wildflowers through National Wildflower Week.

Massachusetts Natural Heritage Program
Division of Fisheries and Wildlife
100 Cambridge St.
Boston, MA 02202
(617)727-9194
A statewide inventory of rare flora, fauna, and plant communities. The program identifies significant natural areas in need of protection and is involved in statewide environmental review.

National Council of State Garden Clubs, Inc.
Operation Wildflower
P. O. Box 860
Pocasset, MA 02559-0860
(617)563-3629
A group that aids in the protection and conservation of natural resources, promotes civic beauty and roadside improvements, advances the fine art of gardening and the study of horticulture, and cooperates with other organizations and agencies.

Nature Conservancy, The
Massachusetts Field Office
201 Devonshire St., 5th Floor
Boston, MA 02110
(617)423-2545
An organization that works for natural land conservation, using acquisition and landowner agreements to maintain the best examples of communities, ecosystems, and endangered species.

New England Botanical Club, Inc.
Harvard University
22 Divinity Ave.
Cambridge, MA 02138
A non-profit organization dedicated to preservation of rare and endangered species in New England.

New England Wild Flower Society
Garden in the Woods
Hemenway Road
Framingham, MA 01701
(508)877-7630
A group founded in 1922 to promote conservation of temperate North American flora through horticulture, education, research, habitat preservation, and advocacy.

Carrie Murray Outdoor Education Campus
Department of Parks and Recreation
1901 Ridgetop Rd.
Baltimore, MD 21207
(301)396-0808
An outdoor education center offering classes, workshops, adventure trips, nature camps, and wildlife rehabilitation programs in a 1,200-acre wilderness park at the western edge of Baltimore.

Cylburn Arboretum Association, Inc.
4015 Greenspring Ave.
Baltimore, MD 21209
(301)367-2217
A group of gardeners who supplement the City of Baltimore in caring for the grounds.

Landon Azalea Garden Festival
Landon School Wildflower Committee
6101 Wilson Lane
Bethesda, MD 20817
(301)320-3200
A festival held the first weekend in May. The committee propagates more than 100 species of wildflowers during the year for sale during the festival.

Maryland Natural Heritage Program
Department of Natural Resources
B-2, Tawes Building
Annapolis, MD 21401
(301)974-2870
A state agency that identifies, lists, manages, and protects rare, threatened, and endangered species.

National Plant Materials Center
USDA, Soil Conservation Service
Building 509, BARC-East
Beltsville, MD 20705
(301)344-2175
A national plant materials center that has a wildflower area and propagates native plants.

Nature Conservancy, The
Maryland Field Office
2 Wisconsin Circle, Suite 600
Chevy Chase, MD 20815
(301)656-8673
An organization that works for natural land conservation, using acquisition and landowner agreements to maintain the best examples of communities, ecosystems, and endangered species.

Wildlife Habitat Enhancement Council
1010 Wayne Ave., Suite 1240
Silver Spring, MD 20910
(301)588-8994
A non-profit organization uniting the corporate and conservation communities to enhance corporate lands to benefit animal and plant life.

Eagle Hill Wildlife Research Station
Dyer Bay Road
Steuben, ME 04680
(207)546-2821
A station offering advanced and professional-level educational programs in botany and other fields.

Maine Natural Heritage Program
State House Station 130
219 Capitol Ave.
Augusta, ME 04333
(207)289-6800
A state agency that identifies, lists, manages, and protects rare, threatened, and endangered species.

Nature Conservancy, The
Maine Chapter
122 Main St.
Topsham, ME 04086
(207)729-5181
An organization that works for natural land conservation, using acquisition and landowner agreements to maintain the best examples of communities, ecosystems, and endangered species.

Beal Botanical Garden of Michigan State University
412 Olds Hall
East Lansing, MI 48824-1047
(517)355-9582
A botanical garden that supports research, teaching, and public education at Michigan State University.

Fernwood Botanic Garden and Nature Center
13988 Rangeline Rd.
Niles, MI 49120
(616)683-8653
A combined nature center, botanic garden, and arts and crafts center.

Hidden Lake Gardens
6820 W. Munger
Tipton, MI 49287
(517)431-2060
An endowed 670-acre public garden featuring both natural and developed landscapes nestled in the scenic Irish Hills of southeast Michigan.

Matthaei Botanical Gardens at The University of Michigan
1800 N. Dixboro Rd.
Ann Arbor, MI 48105
(313)998-7060
A university-related botanical garden of more than 250 acres. The conservatories are the current major public display, but there are outdoor woodland and prairie gardens.

Michigan Botanical Club
Matthaei Botanic Gardens
1800 N. Dixboro Rd.
Ann Arbor, MI 48105
A club that sponsors education, research, and legislative action to promote the preservation of Michigan native flora.

Michigan Natural Features Inventory
P. O. Box 30028
Fifth Floor, Mason Building
Lansing, MI 48909
(517)373-1552
A state agency that maintains a statewide, comprehensive database on endangered, threatened, and special concern plant and animal species and exemplary natural communities.

Michigan Nature Association
7981 Beard Rd., Box 102
Avoca, MI 48006
(313)324-2626

An organization that owns 130 nature sanctuaries covering 6,300 acres in 49 Michigan counties and is run by volunteers without government money. The sanctuaries protect 201 of the state's Endangered, Threatened, and Of Special Concern species. All preserves are open free to the public.

Nature Conservancy, The
Michigan Field Office
2840 E. Grand River, Suite 5
East Lansing, MI 48823
(517)332-1741

An organization that works for natural land conservation, using acquisition and landowner agreements to maintain the best examples of communities, ecosystems, and endangered species.

Rose Lake Plant Materials Center
USDA, Soil Conservation Service
7472 Stoll Rd.
East Lansing, MI 48823-9807
(517)641-6300

A governmental agency that supports the Soil Conservation Service by developing plants and techniques for using plants to solve resource conservation problems.

The Wildflower Association of Michigan
P. O. Box 80527
Lansing, MI 48908-0527

A non-profit association dedicated to education and the enjoyment, conservation, and utilization of native wildflowers. It is an affiliate of the Michigan Audubon Society.

Carpenter Nature Center
12805 St. Croix Trail
Hastings, MN 55033
(612)437-4359
A nature center located on the bluffs of the St. Croix River and concentrating on outdoor education for all ages. Restoration of native plant communities is underway.

Eloise Butler Wildflower Garden and Bird Sanctuary
3800 Bryant Ave. S
Minneapolis, MN 55409-1029
(612)348-5702
A wildflower preserve dedicated to displaying native Minnesota plants, and open April 1 to October 31.

Federated Garden Clubs of Minnesota
HC 74 Box 2415
Hackensack, MN 56452
(218)682-2304
An organization dedicated to the study and preservation of nature and of horticulture and floral design.

Hormel Nature Center
P. O. Box 673
Austin, MN 55912
(507)437-7519
A tax-supported, city-operated nature center supported also by the Hormel Foundation and the Friends of the J.C. Hormel Nature Center.

Kids for Saving Earth
P. O. Box 47247
Plymouth, MN 55447-0247
(612)525-0002
An independent, non-profit organization dedicated to teaching children about the environment through an international network of KSE clubs.

Maplewood Nature Center

2659 E. Seventh St.
Maplewood, MN 55119
(612)738-9383
A center devoted to educating the public.

Minnesota Landscape Arboretum

P. O. Box 39
3675 Arboretum Dr.
Chanhassen, MN 55317
(612)443-2460
An arboretum affiliated with the University of Minnesota providing education in horticulture and landscape design, developing and evaluating plants for Minnesota and the upper Midwest.

Minnesota Native Plant Society

220 Biological Science Center
1445 Gortner Ave.
St. Paul, MN 55108
A society providing monthly presentations, newsletters, field trips, and occasional symposia to facilitate interest in native plants.

Minnesota Natural Heritage Program (Dept. of Natural Resources)

P. O. Box 7
500 Lafayette Rd.
St. Paul, MN 55155-4007
(612)296-4284
A program that conducts research, assesses data, and promotes wise stewardship of the state's native flora.

Nature Conservancy, The

Minnesota Field Office
P. O. Box 110
Minneapolis, MN 55414
(612)331-0750
An organization that works for natural land conservation, using acquisition and landowner agreements to maintain the best examples of communities, ecosystems, and endangered species.

River Bend Nature Center
P. O. Box 265
Faribault, MN 55021
(507)332-7151
A non-profit organization emphasizing nature education and the conservation and preservation of prairie, oak woodlands, and marsh plant and animal species. A three-acre blacksoil prairie adjoins the nature center.

Springbrook Nature Center
100 85th Ave. NE
Fridley, MN 55432
(612)784-3854
A 127-acre municipal park with diverse native habitats and a full-time environmental educational program for varied audiences. The park is managed to maintain native species.

Wood Lake Nature Center
735 Lake Shore Dr.
Richfield, MN 55423
A city-run nature center of 150 acres: 80 acres of wetlands, 10 acres of restored prairie, and 60 acres of woodlands.

Center for Plant Conservation
c/o Missouri Botanic Garden
P. O. Box 299
St. Louis, MO 63166-0299
(314)577-9450
A center dedicated to saving rare and endangered plants native to the U.S. from extinction by coordinating propagation research at regional botanic gardens.

Elsberry Plant Materials Center
USDA, Soil Conservation Service
Rt. 1 Box 9
Elsberry, MO 63343
(314)898-2012
A governmental agency that supports the Soil Conservation Service by utilizing plants, structures, and conservation techniques in farming.

Missouri Botanical Garden
P. O. Box 299
St. Louis, MO 63166
(314)577-5100
A botanical garden that is internationally recognized for its horticultural displays, educational programs, and scientific research. It is the oldest botanical garden in the United States.

Missouri Native Plant Society
P. O. Box 6612
Jefferson City, MO 65102
A society that promotes education and the conservation and preservation of Missouri's native flora through meetings, hikes, workshops, special events, and publications.

Missouri Natural Heritage Inventory
Missouri Department of Conservation
P. O. Box 180
Jefferson City, MO 65102
(314)751-4115
A group that protects, conserves, and enhances non-game resources and natural ecosystems and promotes public understanding, appreciation, and enjoyment of all natural resources.

Missouri Prairie Foundation
P. O. Box 200
Columbia, MO 65205
A non-profit organization concerned with furthering the scientific study, aesthetic appreciation, historical understanding, educational involvement, and preservation of our native grasslands.

Nature Conservancy, The
Missouri Field Office
2800 S. Brentwood Blvd.
St. Louis, MO 63144
(314)968-1105
An organization that works for natural land conservation, using acquisition and landowner agreements to maintain the best examples of communities, ecosystems, and endangered species.

Coffeeville Plant Materials Center
USDA, Soil Conservation Service
Rt. 3 Box 215A
Coffeeville, MS 38922
(601)675-2588
A plant materials center that finds and evaluates plants to solve specific conservation problems, then develops foundation seed sources for commercial seed growers.

Crosby Arboretum, The
3702 Hardy St.
Hattiesburg, MS 39402-1597
(601)261-3137
An arboretum representing the native flora of the Pearl River drainage basin in Mississippi and Louisiana.

Mississippi Native Plant Society
P. O. Box 2151
Starkville, MS 39759
A group promoting the conservation of natural areas through education, meetings, field trips, and native plant propagation.

Mississippi Natural Heritage Program
Museum of Natural Science
111 N. Jefferson St.
Jackson, MS 39201-2897
(601)354-7303
A state agency that identifies, lists, manages, and protects rare, threatened, and endangered species.

Nature Conservancy, The
Mississippi Field Office
P. O. Box 1028
Jackson, MS 39215-1028
(601)355-5357
An organization that works for natural land conservation, using acquisition and landowner agreements to maintain the best examples of communities, ecosystems, and endangered species.

Bridger Plant Materials Center
USDA, Soil Conservation Service
Rt. 1 Box 1189
Bridger, MT 59014-9718
(406)662-3579
A plant materials center that finds and evaluates plants to solve specific conservation problems, then develops foundation seed sources for commercial seed growers.

Montana Native Plant Society
P. O. Box 992
Bozeman, MT 59771
(406)587-0120
A society dedicated to the preservation and study of the native plants and plant communities of Montana and education of the public about the value of native flora.

Montana Natural Heritage Program
State Library Building
1515 E. 6th Ave.
Helena, MT 59620
(406)444-3009
A statewide, computer-assisted inventory of rare and endangered plants and animals and exemplary plant communities.

Nature Conservancy, The
Montana Field Office
P. O. Box 258
Helena, MT 59724
(406)443-0303
An organization that works for natural land conservation, using acquisition and landowner agreements to maintain the best examples of communities, ecosystems, and endangered species.

Nature Conservancy, The
North Carolina Field Office
Carr Mill Mall, Suite 223
Carrboro, NC 27510
(919)967-7007
An organization that works for natural land conservation, using acquisition and landowner agreements to maintain the best examples of communities, ecosystems, and endangered species.

North Carolina Botanical Garden
CB#3375 Totten Center
University of North Carolina at Chapel Hill
Chapel Hill, NC 27599-3375
(919)962-0522
A teaching, research, and public service facility of the University of North Carolina. It is a center for the study, display, interpretation, and conservation of plants and natural areas.

North Carolina Natural Heritage Program
Department of Environment, Health and Natural Resources
P. O. Box 27687
Raleigh, NC 27611
(919)733-7701
A statewide inventory for protection of rare species, habitats, and special natural areas.

North Carolina State University Arboretum, The
Department of Horticulture Science, NCSU
P. O. Box 7609
Raleigh, NC 27695-7609
(919)737-3132
A university arboretum specializing in the evaluation of woody plants for landscape use, distributing promising materials to nurseries for commercial production.

North Carolina Wild Flower Preservation Society, Inc.
c/o North Carolina Botanical Garden
CB#3375, UNC-CH
Chapel Hill, NC 27599-3375
A society to promote enjoyment and conservation of native plants and their habitats through education, protection, and propagation.

Piedmont Environmental Center
1228 Penny Rd.
High Point, NC 27265
(919)454-4214
A non-profit organization committed to environmental education.

Sarah P. Duke Gardens and H. L. Blomquist Garden
Duke University
Durham, NC 27706
(919)684-3698
A landscaped, 6-acre garden of native plants from the southeastern United States.

Southern Appalachian Botanical Club
c/o Janice Coffey Swab, President
Department of Biology, St. Mary's College
Raleigh, NC 27603
(919)828-2521
A club interested in the botany of the Southern Appalachian Mountains.

The Institute of Conservation & Culture
P. O. Box 611
Carrboro, NC 27510
(919)942-1152
A small, non-profit organization dedicated to collaborative education, research, and planning for the integrated health of plants, animals, and people in culturally diverse settings.

University Botanical Gardens at Asheville, Inc.
151 W. T. Weaver Blvd.
Asheville, NC 28804
(704)252-5190
A non-profit association dedicated to the preservation and display of the native flora of Southern Appalachia and the Carolinas and supported by friends and volunteers. The association cares for a 9-acre botanical garden with native flora.

Bismarck Plant Materials Center
USDA, Soil Conservation Service
P. O. Box 1458
Bismarck, ND 58502
(701)223-8536
A plant materials center that finds and evaluates plants to solve specific conservation problems, then develops foundation seed sources for commercial seed growers.

Nature Conservancy, The
Dakotas Field Office
1014 E. Central Ave.
Bismarck, ND 58501
(701)222-8464
An organization that works for natural land conservation, using acquisition and landowner agreements to maintain the best examples of communities, ecosystems, and endangered species.

North Dakota Natural Heritage Inventory
Parks and Recreation Department
1424 W. Century Ave., Suite 202
Bismarck, ND 58501
(701)224-4887
A state agency that identifies, lists, manages, and protects rare, threatened, and endangered species.

Nature Conservancy, The
Nebraska Field Office
418 S. 10th St.
Omaha, NE 68102
(402)342-0282
An organization that works for natural land conservation, using acquisition and landowner agreements to maintain the best examples of communities, ecosystems, and endangered species.

Nebraska Natural Heritage Program, Game and Parks Commission
P. O. Box 30370
2200 N. 33rd St.
Lincoln, NE 68503
(402)471-5421
A state agency that identifies, lists, manages, and protects rare, threatened, and endangered species.

Nebraska Statewide Arboretum
University of Nebraska
Lincoln, NE 68583-0823
(402)472-2971
An arboretum that coordinates 44 affiliated arboreta across Nebraska. It has a membership program and is active in funding community beautification projects.

Prairie/Plains Resource Institute
1307 L St.
Aurora, NE 68818
(402)694-5535
A non-profit organization that works to promote preservation and restoration of native prairie and other unique habitats, promotes public education about regional natural and cultural history, and to develop a center for conservation research and education.

Wayne State College Arboretum
Wayne State College
Wayne, NE 68787
(402)375-2200
A teaching and community arboretum located on the campus of a four-year state college.

Nature Conservancy, The
New Hampshire Field Office
2-1/2 Bacon St., Suite 6
Concord, NH 03301
(603)224-5853
An organization that works for natural land conservation, using acquisition and landowner agreements to maintain the best examples of communities, ecosystems, and endangered species.

New Hampshire Natural Heritage Inventory
Department of Resources and Economic Development
P. O. Box 856
Concord, NH 03302
(603)271-3623
An agency that collects and analyzes data on the status and location of rare or declining native species and exemplary natural communities in the state.

Cape May Plant Materials Center
USDA, Soil Conservation Service
1536 Rt. 9-N
Cape May Court House, NJ 08210
(609)465-5901
A plant materials center that finds and evaluates plants to solve specific conservation problems, then develops foundation seed sources for commercial seed growers.

Morris County Park Commission
P. O. Box 1295
53 East Hanover Ave.
Morristown, NJ 07962-1295
(201)326-7600
An arboretum that manages the Emilie K. Hammond Wildflower Trail at the Tourne Park in Boonton. The trail is a public trail with labeled woodland plants.

Nature Conservancy, The
New Jersey Field Office
17 Fairmont Rd.
Pottersville, NJ 07979
(201)439-3007
An organization that works for natural land conservation, using acquisition and landowner agreements to maintain the best examples of communities, ecosystems, and endangered species.

New Jersey Conservation Foundation
300 Mendham Rd.
Morristown, NJ 07960
(201)539-7540
A non-profit membership organization acting as a land trust to acquire land for public open-space use.

New Jersey Native Plant Society
P. O. Box 1295
Morristown, NJ 07962-1295
(201)377-3956
A group dedicated to encouraging an appreciation of native flora and preserving it for future generations to enjoy. Comprised of both amateurs and professionals, the society offers a variety of programs, field trips, workshops, plant exchanges, and symposia.

New Jersey Natural Heritage Program
Office of Natural Lands Management
501 E. State St., C-N 404
Trenton, NJ 08625
(609)984-1339
A state park service that administers and operates the New Jersey State Park System.

Project SNAP (Save Native American Plants)
459 Easy St.
Howell, NJ 07731
(201)938-3085
A nationwide effort to rescue native plants from bulldozers and transplant them to nature trails and gardens at schools and parks.

Reeves-Reed Arboretum, The
165 Hobart Ave.
Summit, NJ 07901
(908)273-8787
A non-profit environmental institution on an historic 12.5-acre 1889 estate and dedicated to encouraging, through education and the arts, the conservation and appreciation of the plant world.

Center for Holistic Resource Management
800 Rio Grande Blvd. NW, Suite 10
Albuquerque, NM 87104
(505)242-9272
An educational non-profit organization that provides training and consultation in holistic resources management.

Los Lunas Plant Materials Center
USDA, Soil Conservation Service
1036 Miller St. SW
Los Lunas, NM 87031
(505)865-4684
A Soil Conservation Service facility dedicated to testing and developing conservation plant materials.

Native Plant Society of New Mexico
P. O. Box 5917
Santa Fe, NM 87502
(505)434-3041
A society with five local chapters dedicated to promoting the flora of New Mexico through workshops, trips, meetings, and encouraging the use of native and drought-tolerant plants in landscaping.

Nature Conservancy, The
New Mexico Field Office
107 Cienega St.
Santa Fe, NM 87501
(505)988-3867
An organization that works for natural land conservation, using acquisition and landowner agreements to maintain the best examples of communities, ecosystems, and endangered species.

New Mexico Natural Heritage Program
University of New Mexico, Dept. of Biology
2808 Central Ave. SE
Albuquerque, NM 87131
(505)277-1991
A state agency that identifies, lists, manages, and protects rare, threatened, and endangered species.

Public Lands Action Network (PLAN)
P. O. Box 5631
Santa Fe, NM 87502-5631
(505)984-1428
An organization supporting public-land ranching activists with educational tools and networking to fight overgrazing and habitat degradation due to livestock.

Rio Grande Zoological Park
903 10th St. SW
Albuquerque, NM 87102
(505)843-7413
A park exhibiting more than 250 species of animals in naturally landscaped enclosures.

Nature Conservancy, The
Nevada Public Lands Program
133 N. Sierra St., Suite 204
Reno, NV 89501
(702)322-4990
An organization that works for natural land conservation, using acquisition and landowner agreements to maintain the best examples of communities, ecosystems, and endangered species.

Nevada Natural Heritage Program
Division of State Parks
123 W. Nye
Carson City, NV 89710
(702)687-4245
A state agency that identifies, lists, manages, and protects rare, threatened, and endangered species.

Northern Nevada Native Plant Society
P. O. Box 8965
Reno, NV 89507
A society interested in wildflowers, growing native plants, and the conservation of threatened and endangered plants.

Wilbur D. May Arboretum and Botanical Garden
1502 Washington St.
Reno, NV 89503
(702)784-4153
A private arboretum and botanical garden located within Rancho San Rafael Regional Park, a unit of Washoe County Department of Parks and Recreation.

Bayard Cutting Arboretum
P. O. Box 466
Oakdale, NY 11769
(516)581-1002
A public arboretum with major collections of hardy conifers, oaks, hollies, and rhododendrons.

Big Flats Plant Materials Center
USDA, Soil Conservation Service
Box 360A, RR #1, Rt. 352
Corning, NY 14830
(607)562-8404
A plant materials center that develops new conservation plants for problem sites for soil and water conservation.

Cornell Plantations
One Plantations Rd.
Cornell University
Ithaca, NY 14850-2799
(607)256-3020
A museum of living plants set in 200 acres adjacent to the campus and managing nearly 2,000 acres of land as nature preserves.

Federated Garden Clubs of New York State, Inc.
234 Point of Woods Dr.
Albany, NY 12203
(518)869-6311
A non-profit organization interested in conservation and civic beautification. The group promotes youth projects through education, supports garden therapy by working with senior citizens and the handicapped, and studies flower arranging.

Mohonk Preserve, Inc.
Mohonk Lake
New Paltz, NY 12561
(914)255-0919
A privately supported non-profit organization that works to protect an important part of the Shawangunk Mountains and to advance global environmental health based on an appreciation of the interdependence of mankind, nations, and the natural environment.

Nature Conservancy, The
New York Field Office
1736 Western Ave.
Albany, NY 12203
(518)869-6959
An organization that works for natural land conservation, using acquisition and landowner agreements to maintain the best examples of communities, ecosystems, and endangered species.

New York City Department of Parks and Recreation
Attn.: Horticulture Division
1234 Fifth Ave., Arsenal North, 2nd Floor
New York, NY 10029
(212)360-1406
A non-profit organization that plants and maintains city parks, meadows, and park and street trees. The Parks' Natural Resource Group has acquired wetlands areas and other natural areas and maintains a native plant center in Staten Island that rescues rare native species in the area.

New York Natural Heritage Program
Department of Environmental Conservation
700 Troy-Schenectady Rd.
Latham, NY 12110-2400
(518)783-3932
A state agency that inventories and monitors endangered species and is involved with natural habitat management and wildflowers.

Syracuse Botanical Club
c/o Janet Holmes
101 Ambergate Rd.
DeWitt, NY 13214
(315)445-9080
A study group interested in flora of the country and protection of threatened species.

Tifft Nature Preserve
1200 Fuhrmann Blvd.
Buffalo, NY 14203
(716)896-5200
A 264-acre urban nature preserve within the city limits of Buffalo that has been used as a farm, a trans-shipment area, and a dump. It now offers 5-1/2 miles of trails with wildlife, especially water fowl, shorebirds, and songbirds.

Cox Arboretum, The
6733 Springboro Pike
Dayton, OH 45449
(513)454-9005
A landscape arboretum featuring hardy plant materials in a compelling display with 15 specialty gardens.

Dawes Arboretum, The
7770 Jacksontown Rd. SE
Newark, OH 43055
(614)323-2355
A 1,150-acre arboretum exhibiting woody plants hardy to Ohio and maintaining natural habitats of remnant forests.

Holden Arboretum, The
9500 Sperry Rd.
Mentor, OH 44060
(216)256-1110
A 3,200-acre arboretum that is a unique blend of horticultural collections and natural areas. The major collections include rhododendrons, crabapples, lilacs, viburnums, conifers, and wildflowers.

Nature Conservancy, The
Ohio Field Office
1504 W. First Ave.
Columbus, OH 43212
(614)486-6789
An organization that works for natural land conservation, using acquisition and landowner agreements to maintain the best examples of communities, ecosystems, and endangered species.

Ohio Native Plant Society
5 Louise Dr.
Chagrin Falls, OH 44022
(216)338-6622
A group devoted to the preservation and conservation of native plants and plant communities, and the education of the public to the ethics of native plant gardening.

Ohio Natural Heritage Program
Ohio Division of Natural Areas and Preserves
Building F, Fountain Square
Columbus, OH 43224
(614)265-6453
An agency that administers a statewide system of nature preserves and is responsible for the inventory of the state's natural heritage.

Toledo Botanical Garden
P. O. Box 7430
5403 Elmer Dr.
Toledo, OH 43615
(419)536-8365
A botanical garden that displays and demonstrates plant material suitable for northwest Ohio and the Midwest in general.

Nature Conservancy, The
Oklahoma Field Office
320 S. Boston, Suite 1222
Tulsa, OK 74103
(918)585-1117
An organization that works for natural land conservation, using acquisition and landowner agreements to maintain the best examples of communities, ecosystems, and endangered species.

Oklahoma Native Plant Society
2435 S. Peoria Ave.
Tulsa, OK 74114
(918)749-6401
A non-profit society that offers meetings, field trips, a speaker's bureau, and a newsletter to further educate the public about native plants.

Oklahoma Natural Heritage Inventory
Oklahoma Biological Survey
2001 Priestly Ave., Bldg. 605
Norman, OK 73019
(405)325-1985
A state agency that identifies, lists, manages, and protects rare, threatened, and endangered species.

Berry Botanic Garden, The
11505 S.W. Summerville Ave.
Portland, OR 97219
(503)636-4112
A botanic garden committed to scientific, educational, and conservation efforts.

Corvallis Plant Materials Center
USDA, Soil Conservation Service
3420 N.E. Granger Ave.
Corvallis, OR 97330
(503)757-4812
A plant materials center concerned with the assembly, evaluation, and release of plants for conservation purposes. Cultivars are developed for such diverse objectives as streambank stabilization, erosion control, forage, wildlife enhancement, and water quality improvement.

Hoyt Arboretum
4000 S.W. Fairview Blvd.
Portland, OR 97221
(503)228-8732
A display garden of woody plants and an educational center for nature study serving western Oregon and southwestern Washington.

Leach Botanical Garden
6704 S.E. 122nd Ave.
Portland, OR 97236
(503)761-9503
A public botanic garden dedicated to the study of botany and horticulture of the Pacific Northwest and conservation, promotion, and display of these plants.

Mount Pisgah Arboretum
P. O. Box 5621
34909 Frank Parrish Rd.
Eugene, OR 97405
(503)747-3817
An arboretum dedicated to providing the highest quality garden for the public benefit.

Native Plant Society of Oregon
652 W. 10th, #1
Eugene, OR 97402
(503)485-1868
A conservation group dedicated to the study and enjoyment of Oregon's native vegetation.

Nature Conservancy, The
Oregon Field Office
1205 N.W. 25th Ave.
Portland, OR 97210
(503)228-9561
An organization that works for natural land conservation, using acquisition and landowner agreements to maintain the best examples of communities, ecosystems, and endangered species.

Oregon Natural Heritage Program
1205 N.W. 25th Ave.
Portland, OR 97210
(503)229-5078
A state agency that maintains information on rare, threatened, and endangered plants, animal species, and plant communities for the state of Oregon.

Peavy Arboretum and Oregon State University Forests
College of Forestry, Peavy Hall, Room 218
Oregon State University
Corvallis, OR 97331-5711
(503)737-4452 or 737-2608
A part of the University Research Forests, the arboretum is home to 160 species of trees from the Pacific Northwest, the U.S., and the world. The 12,000-acre Research Forests are devoted to research and education.

Xerces Society
10 S.W. Ash St.
Portland, OR 97204
(502)222-2788
An international conservation organization dedicated to preserving rare or endangered invertebrates and their habitats.

Audubon Society of Western Pennsylvania
614 Dorseyville Rd.
Pittsburgh, PA 15238
(412)963-6100
A non-profit environmental education organization.

Bowman's Hill Wildflower Preserve Association
P. O. Box 103
Washington Crossing Historic Park
Washington Crossing, PA 18977
(215)862-2924
An association to support the preserve in furthering its conservation and education mission.

Brandywine Conservancy
P. O. Box 141
Routes U.S. 1 and 100
Chadds Ford, PA 19317
(215)388-7601
A conservancy that seeks to preserve the region's cultural and natural resources. A native plant display garden surrounds the museum and other buildings.

Nature Conservancy, The
Pennsylvania Field Office
1218 Chestnut St., Suite 807
Philadelphia, PA 19107
(215)925-1065
An organization that works for natural land conservation, using acquisition and landowner agreements to maintain the best examples of communities, ecosystems, and endangered species.

Pennsylvania Natural Diversity Inventory
Bureau of Forestry
P. O. Box 8552
Harrisburg, PA 17105
(717)783-0388
A cooperative project of the Pennsylvania Bureau of Forestry, The Nature Conservancy, and the Western Pennsylvania Conservancy, funded primarily from the Wild Resource Conservation Fund, Pennsylvania's income tax check-off fund.

Rodale Research Center
611 Siegfriedale Rd.
Kutztown, PA 19530
(215)683-6383
A non-profit, 305-acre facility where research on organic horticulture and sustainable agriculture is conducted.

Nature Conservancy, The
Rhode Island Field Office
240 Hope St.
Providence, RI 02906
(401)331-7110
An organization that works for natural land conservation, using acquisition and landowner agreements to maintain the best examples of communities, ecosystems, and endangered species.

Rhode Island Natural Heritage Program
Dept. of Environmental Mgmt., Division of Planning and Development
83 Park St.
Providence, RI 02903
(401)277-2776
A state agency involved with the management and monitoring of data regarding rare and endangered plants and animals.

Rhode Island Wild Plant Society
12 Sanderson Rd.
Smithfield, RI 02917
A non-profit conservation organization dedicated to the preservation and protection of Rhode Island's native plants and their habitats.

Brookgreen Gardens
US 17 South
Murrells Inlet, SC 29576
(803)237-4218
An outdoor museum featuring American figurative sculpture placed in landscaped settings. The property is a wildlife sanctuary with native wildlife exhibits that comprise an accredited zoological park.

Nature Conservancy, The
South Carolina Field Office
P. O. Box 5475
Columbia, SC 29250
(803)254-9049
An organization that works for natural land conservation, using acquisition and landowner agreements to maintain the best examples of communities, ecosystems, and endangered species.

South Carolina Heritage Trust
Wildlife and Marine Resources Department
P. O. Box 167
Columbia, SC 29202
(803)734-3893
A state agency that identifies, lists, manages, and protects rare, threatened, and endangered species.

Southern Appalachian Botanical Club

c/o Herbarium, Department of Biology
University of South Carolina
Columbia, SC 29208
A botanical club organized in 1935 to promote botanical interest and to disseminate information concerning the flora and ecology of the southeastern United States.

Wildflower Alliance of South Carolina

P. O. Box 12181
Columbia, SC 29211
(803)799-6889
A group that encourages the protection, propagation, and appreciation of wildflowers and other native plants. The alliance advocates the use of wildflowers on public and private lands for economic and aesthetic value.

Great Plains Botanical Society

P. O. Box 461
Hot Springs, SD 57747-0461
(605)745-3397
A membership organization that studies the flora of the North American Great Plains.

South Dakota Natural Heritage Database

Department of Game, Fish and Parks
523 E. Capitol Ave.
Pierre, SD 57501-3182
(605)773-6245
One of 50 programs in the United States that conducts statewide inventories for rare species and exemplary natural communities.

Chattanooga Nature Center and Reflection Riding

400 Garden Rd.
Chattanooga, TN 37419
(615)821-1160
Two sister organizations, an environmental education center and an arboretum/wildflower preserve, working together for preservation, education, and research.

Cheekwood Botanical Gardens and Fine Arts Center
Forrest Park Drive
Nashville, TN 37205
(615)353-2148
A garden featuring display greenhouses and gardens, including the Howe Wildflower Garden, a center for propagating endangered species.

Dixon Gallery and Gardens
4339 Park Ave.
Memphis, TN 38117
(901)761-5250
An art museum located in a 17-acre woodland display garden.

Ecological Services Division
Tennessee Department of Conservation
701 Broadway
Nashville, TN 37243
(615)742-6545
A state agency that does statewide biological inventory and natural area protection and coordinates department environmental reviews and native plant regulatory programs.

Great Smoky Mountains National Park
Rt. 2
Gatlinburg, TN 37738
A national park and an International Biosphere Reserve.

Native Notes
Rt. 2 Box 550
Heiskell, TN 37754
A newsletter devoted to landscaping with native plants.

Lichterman Nature Center
5992 Quince Rd.
Memphis, TN 38119
(901)685-1566
A 65-acre municipal nature center offering natural history programs, hiking trails, an animal rehab center, and displays for all ages.

Memphis Botanic Garden
750 Cherry Rd.
Memphis, TN 38117
(901)685-1566
A non-profit educational facility featuring 20 plant displays serving as a tourist attraction and tranquil preserve.

Nature Conservancy, The
Tennessee Field Office
226 Capitol Blvd., Suite 202, P. O. Box 3017
Nashville, TN 37219
(615)242-1787
An organization that works for natural land conservation, using acquisition and landowner agreements to maintain the best examples of communities, ecosystems, and endangered species.

Tennessee Native Plant Society
P. O. Box 856
Sewanee, TN 37375-0856
A non-profit native plant society that facilitates information exchange among botanists, and promotes and educates the public about the protection and conservation of native plants.

Warner Park Nature Center
7311 Highway 100
Nashville, TN 37221
(615)352-6299
An environmental education center located on 2,665 acres in the state registry of natural areas.

American Botanical Council
P. O. Box 201660
Austin, TX 78720
(512)331-8868
A non-profit educational organization that distributes information on herbs, herbal research, the historical role and potential for the medical uses of plants, and promotes understanding the importance of preserving native plant populations in temperate and tropical zones.

Chihuahuan Desert Research Institute
P. O. Box 1334
Alpine, TX 79831
(915)837-8370
A non-profit scientific and educational organization that gathers and disseminates information about the Chihuahuan Desert Region.

Corpus Christi Botanical Gardens
8510 S. Staples
Corpus Christi, TX 78413
(512)852-2100
A botanical garden with native and tropical plant displays and a one-mile nature walk. The garden works with three endangered species.

Dallas Arboretum and Botanical Garden
8617 Garland Rd.
Dallas, TX 75218
(214)327-8623
A 65-acre arboretum and botanical garden with two historical homes, open grassy and wildflower areas, and several specialty gardens.

Dallas Nature Center
7575 Wheatland Rd.
Dallas, TX 75249
(214)296-1955
A 400-acre nature center (with 4.5 miles of trails) that works toward conservation, education, research, and recreation.

East Texas Plant Materials Center
USDA, Soil Conservation Service
P. O. Box 13000, SFA Station
Nacogdoches, TX 75962-3000
(409)568-3705
A plant materials center that finds and evaluates plants to solve specific conservation problems, then develops foundation seed sources for commercial seed growers.

El Paso Native Plant Society

c/o James F. George
7137 Gran Vida
El Paso, TX 79912
A society primarily interested in the use of native plants in landscapes to reduce water consumption.

Endangered Resources Branch

Texas Parks and Wildlife Department
4200 Smith School Rd.
Austin, TX 78744
(512)448-4311
A program within the Resource Protection Division of the Texas Parks and Wildlife Department that continually updates information on the status and location of rare species and communities.

Fort Worth Nature Center and Refuge

Rt. 10 Box 53
Fort Worth, TX 76135
(817)237-1111
A non-profit nature center that focuses on environmental education, outdoor recreation, and plant and animal preservation.

Friends of Cibolo Wilderness

P. O. Box 9
Boerne, TX 78006
(512)537-4141
A support organization for the Cibolo Wilderness Trail, a nature preserve in Boerne dedicated to education and preservation.

Heard Natural Science Museum

Rt. 6 Box 22
McKinney, TX 75069
(214)542-5566
A small natural science museum and wildlife sanctuary with exhibits, nature trails, and programs.

Houston Arboretum and Nature Center
4501 Woodway Dr.
Houston, TX 77024
(713)681-8433
An arboretum working to conserve the native plants and animals of Harris County and educate the community about their significance.

Judge Roy Bean Visitor Center
P. O. Box 160
Corner of Loop 25 and Torres Avenue
Langtry, TX 78871
(915)291-3340
An arboretum that maintains the Jersey Lilly Saloon Building, a two-acre cactus garden, and a Texas Travel Information Center with professional travel counselors on duty.

Knox City Plant Materials Center
USDA, Soil Conservation Service
Rt. 1 Box 155
Knox City, TX 79529-9752
(817)658-3922
A plant materials center that evaluates and releases primarily native plant materials useful for a variety of conservation needs.

Mercer Arboretum and Botanic Gardens
22306 Aldine-Westfield Rd.
Humble, TX 77338
(713)443-8731
A 214-acre public botanical garden with extensive natural areas accessed by five miles of trails.

National Wildflower Research Center
2600 F.M. 973 N
Austin, TX 78725-4201
(512)929-3600
A non-profit organization dedicated to the conservation and utilization of the native plants of temperate North America.

Native Plant Project
P. O. Box 1433
Edinburg, TX 78540-1433
A conservation organization dedicated to promoting the use of native plants
and disseminating information about them.

Native Plant Society of Texas
P. O. Box 891
210 W. 8th St., Suite A
Georgetown, TX 78627
A non-profit organization that promotes, conserves, and uses native plants
and their habitats.

Nature Conservancy, The
Texas Field Office
P. O. Box 1440
San Antonio, TX 78295
(512)224-8774
An organization that works for natural land conservation, using acquisition
and landowner agreements to maintain the best examples of communities,
ecosystems, and endangered species.

Riverside Nature Center Association
P. O. Box 645
Kerrville, TX 78029-0645
(512)257-6688
A non-profit organization dedicated to providing information and educa-
tional programs on the natural history of the Texas Hill Country.

Sabal Palm Grove Sanctuary
National Audubon Society
P. O. Box 5052
Brownsville, TX 78523
(512)541-8034
A sanctuary that protects the largest and best preserved remnant of Texas
sabal palm forest left and contains many rare species of plants and animals.

San Antonio Botanical Center
555 Funston
San Antonio, TX 78209
(512)821-5143
A 33-acre public facility with formal gardens, a conservatory complex, and a large area devoted to native Texas plants.

South Texas Plant Materials Center
P. O. Box 218
Texas A&I University
Kingsville, TX 78363
(512)595-2388
A plant materials center that finds and evaluates plants to solve specific conservation problems, then develops foundation seed sources for commercial seed growers.

Texas A & M University Research and Extension Center
1380 A & M Circle
El Paso, TX 79927
(915)859-9111
A project that focuses on arid-land ornamental plants.

Texas Organization for Endangered Species
P. O. Box 12773
Austin, TX 78711-2773
(409)564-7145
An organization working to conserve threatened or endangered species and natural communities.

Valley Land Fund
P. O. Box 2891
McAllen, TX 78502
(512)687-7211
An organization that buys land to protect habitat in the Rio Grande Valley.

Valley Nature Center
P. O. Box 8125
301 S. Border Ave.
Weslaco, TX 78596-8125
(512)969-2475
An environmental education center and museum with a five-acre botanical park.

Wild Basin Wilderness Preserve
P. O. Box 13455
Austin, TX 78711
(512)327-7622
A non-profit organization that manages 227 acres of Hill Country for the preservation of its natural resources through education and research.

Nature Conservancy, The
Great Basin Field Office
P. O. Box 11486
Salt Lake City, UT 84147-0486
(801)531-0999
An organization that works for natural land conservation, using acquisition and landowner agreements to maintain the best examples of communities, ecosystems, and endangered species.

Red Butte Gardens and Arboretum
Building 436
University of Utah
Salt Lake City, UT 84112
(801)581-5322
A new botanical garden fostering an understanding and appreciation of the natural world.

Utah Botanical Gardens
Utah State University
1817 N. Main
Farmington, UT 84025
(801)451-3204
A public display garden located at an Agricultural Experiment Station of Utah State University.

Utah Native Plant Society

P. O. Box 520041
Salt Lake City, UT 84152-0041
(801)581-3744
A native plant society promoting public awareness and education on the conservation of Utah native plants.

Utah Natural Heritage Program

1636 W. N. Temple, Suite 316
Salt Lake City, UT 84116-3193
(801)538-7200
A state program that maintains a continuously updated database of the locations and status of rare plants, rare animals, and natural communities in Utah.

American Horticultural Society

7931 E. Boulevard Dr.
Alexandria, VA 22308
(703)768-5700
A non-profit society promoting horticulture with benefits including educational meetings, publications, seed exchanges, book buyer's service, and a gardener's information service.

Green Spring Farm Park

4603 Green Spring Rd.
Alexandria, VA 22312
(703)642-5173
A 27-acre public garden that is part of the Fairfax County Park Authority. Display and demonstration gardens include native plant, herb, flower, fruit, vegetable, and rock gardens.

Jeffersonia

Biology Department
Bridgewater College
Bridgewater, VA 22812-1599
(703)828-2501
A newsletter for botanists interested in the flora of Virginia.

Maymont Foundation
1700 Hampton St.
Richmond, VA 23228
(804)358-7166
A 105-acre Victorian estate and public park with a formal Italian garden, a Japanese garden, an arboretum, a mansion house, and carriage collection plus domestic and native animals.

Nature Conservancy, The
Science Division Headquarters
1815 North Lynn St.
Arlington, VA 22209
(703)841-5300
An organization that works for natural land conservation, using acquisition and landowner agreements to maintain the best examples of communities, ecosystems, and endangered species.

Nature Conservancy, The
Virginia Field Office
1110 Rose Hill Dr., #200
Charlottesville, VA 22901
(804)295-6106
An organization that works for natural land conservation, using acquisition and landowner agreements to maintain the best examples of communities, ecosystems, and endangered species.

Orland E. White Arboretum
P. O. Box 175
Boyce, VA 22620
(703)837-1758
An arboretum containing diverse woody plant collections of both native and exotic species. Additional native plant collections are planned.

The Winkler Botanical Preserve
4900 Seminary Rd.
Alexandria, VA 22311
(703)578-7888
A preserve located on 43 acres of oak-hickory woodland in an urban setting. Its goal is the cultivation of the native flora of the Potomac Valley drainage in representative habitats.

Virginia Division of Natural Heritage
Department of Conservation and Recreation
203 Governor St., Suite 402
Richmond, VA 23219
(804)786-7951
A state agency that identifies, lists, manages, and protects rare, threatened, and endangered species.

Virginia Federation of Garden Clubs, Inc.
7512 Mayland Dr.
Richmond, VA 23294
(804)270-6301
An organization of 414 garden clubs with 9,607 members.

Virginia Native Plant Society
P. O. Box 844
Annandale, VA 22003
A non-profit organization with eight chapters interested in protecting Virginia's wild plants and habitats, and working to accomplish this goal through natural areas conservation and horticultural and educational efforts.

Nature Conservancy, The
Vermont Field Office
27 State St.
Montpelier, VT 05602-2934
(802)229-4425
An organization that works for natural land conservation, using acquisition and landowner agreements to maintain the best examples of communities, ecosystems, and endangered species.

Vermont Natural Heritage Program
Agency of Natural Resources
Center Building, 103 S. Main St.
Waterbury, VT 05676
(802)244-7340
A program that collects and analyzes data on the status, distribution, and location of rare or declining native species.

Bloedel Reserve, The
7571 N.E. Dolphin Dr.
Bainbridge Island, WA 98110
(206)842-7631
A biological preserve and public garden.

Nature Conservancy, The
Washington Field Office
217 Pine St., Suite 1100
Seattle, WA 98101
(206)343-4344
An organization that works for natural land conservation, using acquisition and landowner agreements to maintain the best examples of communities, ecosystems, and endangered species.

Pullman Plant Materials Center
Room 257, Johnson Hall
Washington State University
Pullman, WA 99164-6428
(509)335-7376
An agency of the Soil Conservation Service, whose role is to develop plants for erosion control.

Rare Plant Consortium
1133 N. Western Ave.
Wenatchee, WA 98801
(509)662-4315
A network of agencies, universities, organizations, and individuals interested in rare plant research and conservation.

Washington Native Plant Society
Department of Botany, KB-15
University of Washington
Seattle, WA 98195
A society that focuses on the native flora of the state of Washington.
Education about and conservation of our flora are the major objectives.

Washington Natural Heritage Program
Department of Natural Resources
Mail Stop EX-13
Olympia, WA 98504
(206)753-2448
An agency that inventories the state for exemplary examples of native
ecosystems and rare plants and maintains a database on their occurrences.

Washington Park Arboretum
University of Washington
XD-10
Seattle, WA 98195
(206)543-8800
A collection of plants managed by the Center for Urban Horticulture, a
cooperative operation of the University of Washington and the City of
Seattle.

Washington State Federation of Garden Clubs
Operation Wildflower
1416 170th Place NE
Bellevue, WA 98008
A group that tries to return the natural heritage of wildflowers to state
roadsides by growing wildflowers from seeds and transplanting them to
Department of Transportation-designated locations and some park areas.

Boerner Botanical Gardens
Milwaukee County Department of Parks
5879 S. 92nd St.
Hales Corners, WI 53130
(414)425-1130
An educational and cultural resource of Milwaukee County that functions as a botanical showplace and an information and resource center to promote proper selection and care of outdoor plant materials.

Botanical Club of Wisconsin
1922 University Ave.
Madison, WI 53705
A club that promotes the appreciation, study, and protection of wild plants and their habitats in Wisconsin through field trips, meetings, and publications.

Bubolz Nature Preserve
4815 N. Lyndale Dr.
Appleton, WI 54915
(414)731-6041
A private, non-profit nature preserve located north of Appleton with the mission of preservation, education, and "silent" recreation.

Calumet Nature Studies, Inc.
P. O. Box 54
Chilton, WI 53014
(414)849-7094
A support group for Ledge View Nature Center, providing volunteers and funds, and organizing special events.

Chiwaukee Prairie Preservation Fund
P. O. Box 1288
Kenosha, WI 53141
(414)637-3141
A group that protects, promotes, and manages the Chiwaukee and Barnes prairies.

International Crane Foundation
E-11376 Shady Lane Rd.
Baraboo, WI 53913
(608)356-9462
A non-profit organization that focuses on the conservation and propogation of cranes worldwide and their habitats. The foundation also has an education department.

Nature Conservancy, The
Wisconsin Field Office
333 W. Mifflin, Suite 107
Madison, WI 53703
(608)251-8140
An organization that works for natural land conservation, using acquisition and landowner agreements to maintain the best examples of communities, ecosystems, and endangered species.

Riveredge Nature Center
4438 W. Hawthorne Dr.
Newburg, WI 53060
(414)931-8095
A private, non-profit environmental education organization dedicated to developing an increased understanding of and concern for the natural environment.

Society for Ecological Restoration
1207 Seminole Highway
Madison, WI 53711
(608)262-9547
A non-profit organization that promotes the exchange of scientific and technological information, and educates its members and the general public about ecosystem restoration. The group is working toward a databank network.

Southwest Wisconsin Prairie Enthusiasts
c/o Gary Eldred
4192 Sleepy Hollow Rd.
Boscobel, WI 53805
(608)375-5271
A group dedicated to purchasing and preserving or managing prairie remnants in southwest Wisconsin.

University of Wisconsin Arboretum
1207 Seminole Highway
Madison, WI 53711
(608)262-2748
An outdoor research and teaching laboratory of the University that specializes in ecological restoration. It features restorations of Wisconsin's native plant communities.

Wehr Nature Center
9701 W. College Ave.
Franklin, WI 53132
(414)425-8550
An environmental education facility of the Milwaukee County Park System.

WILD ONES Natural Landscaping Club
9701 North Lake Dr.
Milwaukee, WI 53217
(414)352-0734
A group that meets to learn about natural landscaping and sponsors seminars, plant digs and sales, and tours of natural yards.

Wisconsin Natural Heritage Inventory
Department of Natural Resources
101 S. Webster St., Box 7921
Madison, WI 53707
(608)266-0924
A state agency that serves as the storehouse of information on rare plant and animal species and natural communities in Wisconsin.

Wisconsin Wetlands Association
c/o Brian Perry
222 S. Hamilton, Suite #1
Madison, WI 53703
(608)251-2252
An organization that promotes appropriate relationships between people and wetlands, focusing on monitoring wetland legislation and public education.

Nature Conservancy, The
West Virginia Field Office
922 Quarrier St., Suite 414
Charleston, WV 25301
(304)345-4350
An organization that works for natural land conservation, using acquisition and landowner agreements to maintain the best examples of communities, ecosystems, and endangered species.

West Virginia Division of Natural Resources/Operation Wildflower
Office of Conservation Education
State Capitol Complex, Bldg 3, Rm 729
Charleston, WV 25305
A state agency charged with protecting the environment.

West Virginia Natural Heritage Program
Department of Natural Resources
P. O. Box 67
Elkins, WV 26241
(304)637-0245
A cooperative enterprise with The Nature Conservancy to maintain a database of locations of rare, threatened, or endangered species and natural communities and to act as a clearinghouse of natural history information of West Virginia.

Nature Conservancy, The
Wyoming Field Office
258 Main St., P. O. Box 450
Lander, WY 82520
(307)332-2971
An organization that works for natural land conservation, using acquisition and landowner agreements to maintain the best examples of communities, ecosystems, and endangered species.

Wyoming Native Plant Society
P. O. Box 1471
Cheyenne, WY 82003-1471
A society dedicated to encouraging the appreciation and conservation of the native plants and ecosystems of Wyoming.

Wyoming Natural Diversity Database
3165 University Station
Laramie, WY 82071
(307)766-3441
A state agency that keeps a computerized inventory of species and natural areas of concern in Wyoming.

Silphium
laciniatum

Native Plant
Nurseries & Seed Companies

Baldwin Seed Company of Alaska
P. O. Box 3127
Kenai, AK 99611-3127
(906)262-2285
Percentage of the business in native species: 100%
Is a catalog or plant list available: Yes
What is the catalog fee, if any: $1.50
Type of business: Retail (x); Wholesale (x); Mail Order (x)
Primary plant focus: Trees & shrubs; Herbaceous wildflowers; Grass seed; Wildflower seed (x); Cacti or succulents

Holland Wildflower Farm
290 O'Neal Lane
Elkins, AR 72727
(501)643-2622
Percentage of the business in native species: 75%
Is a catalog or plant list available: Yes
What is the catalog fee, if any: $1.00
Type of business: Retail (x); Wholesale; Mail Order (x)
Primary plant focus: Trees & shrubs; Herbaceous wildflowers (x); Grass seed; Wildflower seed (x); Cacti or succulents

Cactus World
2955 E. Chula Vista Dr.
Tucson, AZ 85716
(602)795-6028
Percentage of the business in native species: 100%
Is a catalog or plant list available: Yes
What is the catalog fee, if any: SASE
Type of business: Retail; Wholesale (x); Mail Order
Primary plant focus: Trees & shrubs; Herbaceous wildflowers; Grass seed; Wildflower seed; Cacti or succulents (x)

Desert Enterprises
P. O. Box 23
25202 W. Rockaway Hill Dr.
Morristown, AZ 85342
(602)388-2448
Percentage of the business in native species: 100%
Is a catalog or plant list available: Yes
What is the catalog fee, if any: N/A
Type of business: Retail; Wholesale (x); Mail Order (x)
Primary plant focus: Trees & shrubs (x); Herbaceous wildflowers; Grass seed (x); Wildflower seed (x); Cacti or succulents (x)

Lone Mountain Nurseries, Inc.
21515 W. Lone Mountain Road
Wittman, AZ 85361
(602)256-6414
Percentage of the business in native species: 10%
Is a catalog or plant list available: Yes
What is the catalog fee, if any: N/A
Type of business: Retail; Wholesale (x); Mail Order
Primary plant focus: Trees & shrubs (x); Herbaceous wildflowers (x);
Grass seed; Wildflower seed; Cacti or succulents (x)

Mountain States Wholesale Nursery
P. O. Box 33982
Phoenix, AZ 85067
(602)247-8509
Percentage of the business in native species: 90%
Is a catalog or plant list available: Yes
What is the catalog fee, if any: N/A
Type of business: Retail; Wholesale (x); Mail Order
Primary plant focus: Trees & shrubs (x); Herbaceous wildflowers (x);
Grass seed (x); Wildflower seed; Cacti or succulents

Southwestern Native Seeds
P. O. Box 50503
Tucson, AZ 85703
Percentage of the business in native species: 100%
Is a catalog or plant list available: Yes
What is the catalog fee, if any: $1.00
Type of business: Retail (x); Wholesale; Mail Order (x)
Primary plant focus: Trees & shrubs (x); Herbaceous wildflowers (x);
Grass seed; Wildflower seed (x); Cacti or succulents (x)

Starr Nursery
50 E. Blacklidge
Tucson, AZ 85705
(602)628-8773
Percentage of the business in native species: 50%
Is a catalog or plant list available: No
What is the catalog fee, if any:
Type of business: Retail (x); Wholesale (x); Mail Order
Primary plant focus: Trees & shrubs (x); Herbaceous wildflowers (x);
Grass seed; Wildflower seed; Cacti or succulents

Wild Seed, Inc.
P. O. Box 27751
Tempe, AZ 85285
(602)968-9751
Percentage of the business in native species: 90%
Is a catalog or plant list available: Yes
What is the catalog fee, if any: N/A
Type of business: Retail (x); Wholesale (x); Mail Order (x)
Primary plant focus: Trees & shrubs (x); Herbaceous wildflowers (x);
Grass seed (x); Wildflower seed (x); Cacti or succulents (x)

Albright Seed Company
184-A Arthur Road
Martinez, CA 94553
(415)372-8245
Percentage of the business in native species: 10%
Is a catalog or plant list available: Yes
What is the catalog fee, if any: N/A
Type of business: Retail; Wholesale (x); Mail Order
Primary plant focus: Trees & shrubs (x); Herbaceous wildflowers; Grass
seed (x); Wildflower seed (x); Cacti or succulents

Anderson Valley Nursery
18151 Mountain View Rd.
P. O. Box 504
Boonville, CA 95415
(707)895-3853
Percentage of the business in native species: 50%
Is a catalog or plant list available: Yes
What is the catalog fee, if any: N/A
Type of business: Retail (x); Wholesale (x); Mail Order
Primary plant focus: Trees & shrubs (x); Herbaceous wildflowers (x);
Grass seed; Wildflower seed; Cacti or succulents

Bay Area Succulents
6556 Shattuck Ave.
Oakland, CA 94609
(415)547-3564
Percentage of the business in native species: 25%
Is a catalog or plant list available: No
What is the catalog fee, if any:
Type of business: Retail (x); Wholesale; Mail Order
Primary plant focus: Trees & shrubs (x); Herbaceous wildflowers (x);
Grass seed (x); Wildflower seed; Cacti or succulents (x)

Berkeley Horticultural Nursery
1310 McGee Ave.
Berkeley, CA 94703
(415)526-4704
Percentage of the business in native species: 5%
Is a catalog or plant list available: No
What is the catalog fee, if any:
Type of business: Retail (x); Wholesale; Mail Order
Primary plant focus: Trees & shrubs (x); Herbaceous wildflowers (x);
Grass seed (x); Wildflower seed (x); Cacti or succulents (x)

Blue Oak Nursery
2731 Mountain Oak Lane
Rescue, CA 95672
(916)677-2111
Percentage of the business in native species: 60%
Is a catalog or plant list available: Yes
What is the catalog fee, if any: N/A
Type of business: Retail (x); Wholesale (x); Mail Order (x)
Primary plant focus: Trees & shrubs (x); Herbaceous wildflowers; Grass
seed; Wildflower seed; Cacti or succulents

C. H. Baccus
900 Boynton Ave.
San Jose, CA 95117
(408)244-2923
Percentage of the business in native species: 100%
Is a catalog or plant list available: Yes
What is the catalog fee, if any: SASE
Type of business: Retail (x); Wholesale; Mail Order (x)
Primary plant focus: Trees & shrubs; Herbaceous wildflowers (x); Grass
seed; Wildflower seed; Cacti or succulents

Calaveras Nursery
1622 Highway 12
Valley Springs, CA 95252
(209)772-1823
Percentage of the business in native species: 80%
Is a catalog or plant list available: Yes
What is the catalog fee, if any: N/A
Type of business: Retail; Wholesale (x); Mail Order
Primary plant focus: Trees & shrubs (x); Herbaceous wildflowers; Grass
seed; Wildflower seed; Cacti or succulents

California Flora Nursery
P. O. Box 3
Fulton, CA 95439
(707)528-8813
Percentage of the business in native species: 50%
Is a catalog or plant list available: Yes
What is the catalog fee, if any: Free
Type of business: Retail (x); Wholesale (x); Mail Order
Primary plant focus: Trees & shrubs (x); Herbaceous wildflowers (x); Grass seed (x); Wildflower seed; Cacti or succulents

Carter Seeds
475 Mar Vista Dr.
Vista, CA 92083
(619)724-5931
Percentage of the business in native species: 20%
Is a catalog or plant list available: Yes
What is the catalog fee, if any: N/A
Type of business: Retail (x); Wholesale (x); Mail Order (x)
Primary plant focus: Trees & shrubs (x); Herbaceous wildflowers; Grass seed (x); Wildflower seed (x); Cacti or succulents

Circuit Rider Productions
9619 Old Redwood Highway
Windsor, CA 95492
(707)838-6641
Percentage of the business in native species: 100%
Is a catalog or plant list available: Yes
What is the catalog fee, if any: N/A
Type of business: Retail; Wholesale (x); Mail Order
Primary plant focus: Trees & shrubs (x); Herbaceous wildflowers (x); Grass seed (x); Wildflower seed; Cacti or succulents

Clotilde Merlo Forest Tree Nursery
Louisiana-Pacific Corporation
1508 Crannell Road
Trinidad, CA 95570
(707)677-0911
Percentage of the business in native species: 99%
Is a catalog or plant list available: Yes
What is the catalog fee, if any: N/A
Type of business: Retail (x); Wholesale (x); Mail Order (x)
Primary plant focus: Trees & shrubs (x); Herbaceous wildflowers; Grass seed; Wildflower seed; Cacti or succulents

Clyde Robin Seed Co., Inc.
3670 Enterprise Ave.
Hayward, CA 94545
(415)785-9425
Percentage of the business in native species: 80%
Is a catalog or plant list available: Yes
What is the catalog fee, if any: N/A
Type of business: Retail (x); Wholesale (x); Mail Order (x)
Primary plant focus: Trees & shrubs (x); Herbaceous wildflowers; Grass seed (x); Wildflower seed (x); Cacti or succulents

Conservaseed
P. O. Box 455
Rio Vista, CA 94571
(916)775-1646
Percentage of the business in native species: 75%
Is a catalog or plant list available: Yes
What is the catalog fee, if any: N/A
Type of business: Retail; Wholesale (x); Mail Order
Primary plant focus: Trees & shrubs; Herbaceous wildflowers; Grass seed (x); Wildflower seed; Cacti or succulents

Cornflower Farms
P. O. Box 896
Elk Grove, CA 95759
(916)689-1015
Percentage of the business in native species: 80-90%
Is a catalog or plant list available: Yes
What is the catalog fee, if any: N/A
Type of business: Retail; Wholesale (x); Mail Order
Primary plant focus: Trees & shrubs (x); Herbaceous wildflowers; Grass seed (x); Wildflower seed; Cacti or succulents

Design Associates Working with Nature
1442-A Walnut St. Box 101
Berkeley, CA 94709
(415)527-5659
Percentage of the business in native species: 100%
Is a catalog or plant list available: Yes
What is the catalog fee, if any: SASE
Type of business: Retail (x); Wholesale; Mail Order
Primary plant focus: Trees & shrubs (x); Herbaceous wildflowers (x); Grass seed (x); Wildflower seed; Cacti or succulents (x)

Environmental Seed Producers, Inc.
P. O. Box 2709
1851 W. Olive Ave.
Lompoc, CA 93438-2709
(805)735-8888
Percentage of the business in native species: 50%
Is a catalog or plant list available: Yes
What is the catalog fee, if any: N/A
Type of business: Retail; Wholesale (x); Mail Order
Primary plant focus: Trees & shrubs; Herbaceous wildflowers; Grass seed; Wildflower seed (x); Cacti or succulents

Grasslands Nursery
2222 Third St. (at Bancroft)
Berkeley, CA 94710
(510)540-8011
Percentage of the business in native species: 60-70%
Is a catalog or plant list available: Yes
What is the catalog fee, if any: Free
Type of business: Retail (x); Wholesale (x); Mail Order
Primary plant focus: Trees & shrubs (x); Herbaceous wildflowers (x);
Grass seed (x); Wildflower seed (x); Cacti or succulents

Hacienda Hay
P. O. Box 222435
Carmel, CA 93922
(408)624-5119
Percentage of the business in native species: N/A
Is a catalog or plant list available: No
What is the catalog fee, if any:
Type of business: Retail (x); Wholesale; Mail Order
Primary plant focus: Trees & shrubs (x); Herbaceous wildflowers (x);
Grass seed (x); Wildflower seed (x); Cacti or succulents

Hardscrabble Seed Co.
Rt. 2 Box 255
Springville, CA 93265
(209)539-3593
Percentage of the business in native species: 100%
Is a catalog or plant list available: Yes
What is the catalog fee, if any: N/A
Type of business: Retail; Wholesale (x); Mail Order (x)
Primary plant focus: Trees & shrubs (x); Herbaceous wildflowers; Grass
seed; Wildflower seed; Cacti or succulents

J. L. Hudson, Seedsman
P. O. Box 1058
Redwood City, CA 94064
Percentage of the business in native species: 90%
Is a catalog or plant list available: Yes
What is the catalog fee, if any: $1.00
Type of business: Retail (x); Wholesale (x); Mail Order (x)
Primary plant focus: Trees & shrubs (x); Herbaceous wildflowers (x);
Grass seed (x); Wildflower seed (x); Cacti or succulents (x)

Larner Seeds
P. O. Box 407
Bolinas, CA 94924
(415)868-9407
Percentage of the business in native species: 99%
Is a catalog or plant list available: Yes
What is the catalog fee, if any: $1.50
Type of business: Retail (x); Wholesale (x); Mail Order (x)
Primary plant focus: Trees & shrubs (x); Herbaceous wildflowers (x);
Grass seed (x); Wildflower seed (x); Cacti or succulents

Living Desert, The
47900 Portola Ave.
Palm Desert, CA 92260
(619)346-5694
Percentage of the business in native species: 80%
Is a catalog or plant list available: Yes
What is the catalog fee, if any: N/A
Type of business: Retail (x); Wholesale (x); Mail Order
Primary plant focus: Trees & shrubs (x); Herbaceous wildflowers; Grass
seed (x); Wildflower seed; Cacti or succulents (x)

Mockingbird Nurseries, Inc.
1670 Jackson St.
Riverside, CA 92504
(714)780-3571
Percentage of the business in native species: 95%
Is a catalog or plant list available: Yes
What is the catalog fee, if any: N/A
Type of business: Retail; Wholesale (x); Mail Order
Primary plant focus: Trees & shrubs (x); Herbaceous wildflowers (x); Grass seed; Wildflower seed; Cacti or succulents

Moon Mountain Wildflowers
P. O. Box 34
Morro Bay, CA 93443
(805)772-2473
Percentage of the business in native species: 50%
Is a catalog or plant list available: Yes
What is the catalog fee, if any: $2.00
Type of business: Retail (x); Wholesale (x); Mail Order (x)
Primary plant focus: Trees & shrubs; Herbaceous wildflowers; Grass seed; Wildflower seed (x); Cacti or succulents

Mostly Natives Nursery
P. O. Box 258
27215 Highway 1
Tomales, CA 94971
(707)878-2009
Percentage of the business in native species: 50%
Is a catalog or plant list available: Yes
What is the catalog fee, if any: N/A
Type of business: Retail (x); Wholesale (x); Mail Order
Primary plant focus: Trees & shrubs (x); Herbaceous wildflowers (x); Grass seed (x); Wildflower seed; Cacti or succulents

Native Sons Wholesale Nursery
379 W. El Campo Road
Arroyo Grande, CA 93420
(805)481-5996
Percentage of the business in native species: 50%
Is a catalog or plant list available: Yes
What is the catalog fee, if any: $1.00
Type of business: Retail; Wholesale (x); Mail Order
Primary plant focus: Trees & shrubs (x); Herbaceous wildflowers (x);
Grass seed (x); Wildflower seed; Cacti or succulents (x)

Pacific Coast Seed, Inc.
7074-D Commerce Circle
Pleasanton, CA 94588
(510)463-1188
Percentage of the business in native species: 50-60%
Is a catalog or plant list available: Yes
What is the catalog fee, if any: Free
Type of business: Retail; Wholesale (x); Mail Order
Primary plant focus: Trees & shrubs (x); Herbaceous wildflowers; Grass
seed (x); Wildflower seed (x); Cacti or succulents

Pacific Southwest Nursery
P. O. Box 985
National City, CA 91951-9085
(619)477-5333
Percentage of the business in native species: 100%
Is a catalog or plant list available: Yes
What is the catalog fee, if any: Free
Type of business: Retail; Wholesale (x); Mail Order
Primary plant focus: Trees & shrubs (x); Herbaceous wildflowers (x);
Grass seed (x); Wildflower seed (x); Cacti or succulents

Redwood City Seed Company
P. O. Box 361
Redwood City, CA 94064
(415)325-7333
Percentage of the business in native species: 100%
Is a catalog or plant list available: Yes
What is the catalog fee, if any: Three first-class stamps
Type of business: Retail (x); Wholesale (x); Mail Order (x)
Primary plant focus: Trees & shrubs; Herbaceous wildflowers; Grass seed (x); Wildflower seed (x); Cacti or succulents

S & S Seeds
P. O. Box 1275
Carpinteria, CA 93013
(805)684-0436
Percentage of the business in native species: 80%
Is a catalog or plant list available: Yes
What is the catalog fee, if any: N/A
Type of business: Retail; Wholesale (x); Mail Order
Primary plant focus: Trees & shrubs (x); Herbaceous wildflowers; Grass seed (x); Wildflower seed (x); Cacti or succulents

San Simeon Nursery
Villa Creek Road
Cayucos, CA 93430
(805)995-2466
Percentage of the business in native species: 40%
Is a catalog or plant list available: Yes
What is the catalog fee, if any: N/A
Type of business: Retail; Wholesale (x); Mail Order
Primary plant focus: Trees & shrubs (x); Herbaceous wildflowers (x); Grass seed (x); Wildflower seed; Cacti or succulents (x)

Saratoga Horticultural Foundation
15185 Murphy Ave.
San Martin, CA 95046
(408)779-3303
Percentage of the business in native species: 30%
Is a catalog or plant list available: Yes
What is the catalog fee, if any: N/A
Type of business: Retail; Wholesale (x); Mail Order
Primary plant focus: Trees & shrubs (x); Herbaceous wildflowers; Grass seed; Wildflower seed; Cacti or succulents

Skylark Wholesale Nursery
6735 Sonoma Highway
Santa Rosa, CA 95409
(707)539-1565
Percentage of the business in native species: 30%
Is a catalog or plant list available: Yes
What is the catalog fee, if any: N/A
Type of business: Retail; Wholesale (x); Mail Order
Primary plant focus: Trees & shrubs (x); Herbaceous wildflowers (x); Grass seed; Wildflower seed; Cacti or succulents

Theodore Payne Foundation
10459 Tuxford St.
Sun Valley, CA 91352
(818)768-1802
Percentage of the business in native species: 100%
Is a catalog or plant list available: Yes
What is the catalog fee, if any: $2.00
Type of business: Retail (x); Wholesale; Mail Order (x)
Primary plant focus: Trees & shrubs (x); Herbaceous wildflowers (x); Grass seed (x); Wildflower seed (x); Cacti or succulents (x)

Tree of Life Nursery
P. O. Box 736
San Juan Capistrano, CA 92693
(714)728-0685
Percentage of the business in native species: 100%
Is a catalog or plant list available: Yes
What is the catalog fee, if any: $3.50
Type of business: Retail; Wholesale (x); Mail Order
Primary plant focus: Trees & shrubs (x); Herbaceous wildflowers (x); Grass seed (x); Wildflower seed (x); Cacti or succulents (x)

Wapumne Native Plant Nursery Co.
3807 Mt. Pleasant Road
Lincoln, CA 95648
(916)645-9737
Percentage of the business in native species: 100%
Is a catalog or plant list available: N/A
What is the catalog fee, if any:
Type of business: Retail (x); Wholesale (x); Mail Order
Primary plant focus: Trees & shrubs (x); Herbaceous wildflowers (x); Grass seed (x); Wildflower seed; Cacti or succulents

Weber Nursery
237 Seeman Dr.
Encinitas, CA 92024
(619)753-1661
Percentage of the business in native species: 99%
Is a catalog or plant list available: Yes
What is the catalog fee, if any: $1.00 + SASE with two stamps
Type of business: Retail (x); Wholesale; Mail Order
Primary plant focus: Trees & shrubs (x); Herbaceous wildflowers; Grass seed; Wildflower seed; Cacti or succulents (x)

Western Hills Nursery
16250 Coleman Valley Road
Occidental, CA 95465
(707)874-3731
Percentage of the business in native species: 25%
Is a catalog or plant list available: Yes
What is the catalog fee, if any: $2.00
Type of business: Retail (x); Wholesale; Mail Order
Primary plant focus: Trees & shrubs (x); Herbaceous wildflowers (x);
Grass seed (x); Wildflower seed; Cacti or succulents

Wildflowers International, Inc.
P. O. Box 131
Elk, CA 95432
(707)877-3400
Percentage of the business in native species: 50%
Is a catalog or plant list available: Yes
What is the catalog fee, if any: N/A
Type of business: Retail; Wholesale (x); Mail Order
Primary plant focus: Trees & shrubs; Herbaceous wildflowers; Grass
seed; Wildflower seed (x); Cacti or succulents

Wildwood Farm
10300 Sonoma Highway
Kenwood, CA 95452
(707)833-1161
Percentage of the business in native species: 50%
Is a catalog or plant list available: Yes
What is the catalog fee, if any: $1.00
Type of business: Retail (x); Wholesale (x); Mail Order (x)
Primary plant focus: Trees & shrubs (x); Herbaceous wildflowers (x);
Grass seed (x); Wildflower seed; Cacti or succulents

YA-KA-AMA Native Plant Nursery
6215 Eastside Road
Forestville, CA 95436
(707)887-1541
Percentage of the business in native species: 70%
Is a catalog or plant list available: Yes
What is the catalog fee, if any: N/A
Type of business: Retail; Wholesale (x); Mail Order
Primary plant focus: Trees & shrubs (x); Herbaceous wildflowers (x); Grass seed (x); Wildflower seed (x); Cacti or succulents

Yerba Buena Nursery
19500 Skyline Blvd.
Woodside, CA 94062
(415)851-1668
Percentage of the business in native species: 90%
Is a catalog or plant list available: Yes
What is the catalog fee, if any: N/A
Type of business: Retail (x); Wholesale; Mail Order
Primary plant focus: Trees & shrubs (x); Herbaceous wildflowers (x); Grass seed (x); Wildflower seed (x); Cacti or succulents (x)

Applewood Seed Co.
5380 Vivian
Arvada, CO 80002
(303)431-6283
Percentage of the business in native species: 70%
Is a catalog or plant list available: Yes
What is the catalog fee, if any: N/A
Type of business: Retail; Wholesale (x); Mail Order
Primary plant focus: Trees & shrubs; Herbaceous wildflowers (x); Grass seed; Wildflower seed (x); Cacti or succulents

Arkansas Valley Seed Co.
4625 Colorado Blvd.
Denver, CO 80216
(303)254-7469
Percentage of the business in native species: 20%
Is a catalog or plant list available: No
What is the catalog fee, if any:
Type of business: Retail; Wholesale (x); Mail Order
Primary plant focus: Trees & shrubs; Herbaceous wildflowers; Grass seed (x); Wildflower seed (x); Cacti or succulents

Currents Company
P. O. Box 2608
Telluride, CO 81435
(303)728-3250
Percentage of the business in native species: 100%
Is a catalog or plant list available: Yes
What is the catalog fee, if any: N/A
Type of business: Retail; Wholesale (x); Mail Order
Primary plant focus: Trees & shrubs; Herbaceous wildflowers; Grass seed; Wildflower seed (x); Cacti or succulents

Dean Swift Seed Company
P. O. Box B
Jaroso, CO 81138
(303)672-3739
Percentage of the business in native species: 99%
Is a catalog or plant list available: Yes
What is the catalog fee, if any: N/A
Type of business: Retail; Wholesale (x); Mail Order (x)
Primary plant focus: Trees & shrubs; Herbaceous wildflowers; Grass seed; Wildflower seed (x); Cacti or succulents

Edge of the Rockies
133 Hunna Road
Bayfield, CO 81122-9758
Percentage of the business in native species: 100%
Is a catalog or plant list available: Yes
What is the catalog fee, if any: $1.00
Type of business: Retail (x); Wholesale; Mail Order (x)
Primary plant focus: Trees & shrubs (x); Herbaceous wildflowers (x); Grass seed (x); Wildflower seed (x); Cacti or succulents

Neils Lunceford, Inc.
P. O. Box 102
Dillon, CO 80435
(303)468-0340
Percentage of the business in native species: 40%
Is a catalog or plant list available: No
What is the catalog fee, if any:
Type of business: Retail (x); Wholesale; Mail Order
Primary plant focus: Trees & shrubs (x); Herbaceous wildflowers (x); Grass seed (x); Wildflower seed (x); Cacti or succulents (x)

Rocky Mountain Rare Plants
P. O. Box 20483
Denver, CO 80220-0483
Percentage of the business in native species: 95%
Is a catalog or plant list available: Yes
What is the catalog fee, if any: $1.00
Type of business: Retail (x); Wholesale (x); Mail Order (x)
Primary plant focus: Trees & shrubs; Herbaceous wildflowers (x); Grass seed; Wildflower seed (x); Cacti or succulents

Southwest Seed, Inc.
13260 Ct. Rd. 29
Dolores, CO 81323
(303)565-8722
Percentage of the business in native species: 40%
Is a catalog or plant list available: Yes
What is the catalog fee, if any: Free
Type of business: Retail; Wholesale (x); Mail Order
Primary plant focus: Trees & shrubs; Herbaceous wildflowers (x); Grass seed (x); Wildflower seed (x); Cacti or succulents

Western Native Seed
P. O. Box 1281
Canon City, CO 81215
(719)275-8414
Percentage of the business in native species: 100%
Is a catalog or plant list available: Yes
What is the catalog fee, if any: $1.00
Type of business: Retail (x); Wholesale (x); Mail Order (x)
Primary plant focus: Trees & shrubs; Herbaceous wildflowers; Grass seed; Wildflower seed (x); Cacti or succulents

Wild and Crazy Seed Co.
P. O. Box 895
Durango, CO 81302
(303)247-4827
Percentage of the business in native species: 100%
Is a catalog or plant list available: Yes
What is the catalog fee, if any: $1.00
Type of business: Retail; Wholesale (x); Mail Order (x)
Primary plant focus: Trees & shrubs (x); Herbaceous wildflowers (x); Grass seed (x); Wildflower seed (x); Cacti or succulents

Wild Things
218 Quincy
Pueblo, CO 81004
(719)543-2722
Percentage of the business in native species: 100%
Is a catalog or plant list available: Yes
What is the catalog fee, if any: Free
Type of business: Retail; Wholesale (x); Mail Order
Primary plant focus: Trees & shrubs; Herbaceous wildflowers (x); Grass seed; Wildflower seed; Cacti or succulents

Birdsong Nursery
511 Royal Oak Road
Webster, FL 33597
(904)793-4244
Percentage of the business in native species: 40%
Is a catalog or plant list available: Yes
What is the catalog fee, if any: Free
Type of business: Retail (x); Wholesale (x); Mail Order (x)
Primary plant focus: Trees & shrubs (x); Herbaceous wildflowers; Grass seed; Wildflower seed; Cacti or succulents

Blake's Nursery
Rt. 2 Box 971
Highway 90 East
Madison, FL 32340
(904)971-5003
Percentage of the business in native species: 80-90%
Is a catalog or plant list available: Yes
What is the catalog fee, if any: Free
Type of business: Retail (x); Wholesale (x); Mail Order (x)
Primary plant focus: Trees & shrubs (x); Herbaceous wildflowers; Grass seed; Wildflower seed; Cacti or succulents

Breezy Oaks Nursery
Route 4 Box 6-A
Hawthorn, FL 32640
(904)481-3795
Percentage of the business in native species: 40%
Is a catalog or plant list available: No
What is the catalog fee, if any:
Type of business: Retail (x); Wholesale (x); Mail Order
Primary plant focus: Trees & shrubs (x); Herbaceous wildflowers (x);
Grass seed (x); Wildflower seed; Cacti or succulents

Bullbay Creek Farm
Rt. 2 Box 381
Tallahassee, FL 32301
(904)878-6688
Percentage of the business in native species: 90%
Is a catalog or plant list available: Yes
What is the catalog fee, if any: N/A
Type of business: Retail; Wholesale (x); Mail Order
Primary plant focus: Trees & shrubs (x); Herbaceous wildflowers (x);
Grass seed (x); Wildflower seed; Cacti or succulents

Central Florida Lands & Timber, Inc.
Rt. 1 Box 899
Mayo, FL 32066
(904)294-1211
Percentage of the business in native species: 100%
Is a catalog or plant list available: Yes
What is the catalog fee, if any: N/A
Type of business: Retail; Wholesale (x); Mail Order (x)
Primary plant focus: Trees & shrubs (x); Herbaceous wildflowers (x);
Grass seed; Wildflower seed; Cacti or succulents

Central Florida Native Flora, Inc.
P. O. Box 1045
San Antonio, FL 33576-1045
(904)588-3687
Percentage of the business in native species: 100%
Is a catalog or plant list available: Yes
What is the catalog fee, if any: Free
Type of business: Retail; Wholesale (x); Mail Order
Primary plant focus: Trees & shrubs (x); Herbaceous wildflowers (x);
Grass seed (x); Wildflower seed; Cacti or succulents

Dan's Native Nursery
2325 Lake Easy Road
Babson Park, FL 33827
(813)638-1203
Percentage of the business in native species: 99%
Is a catalog or plant list available: Yes
What is the catalog fee, if any: Free
Type of business: Retail (x); Wholesale (x); Mail Order
Primary plant focus: Trees & shrubs (x); Herbaceous wildflowers; Grass
seed; Wildflower seed; Cacti or succulents

Ecohorizons, Inc.
22601 S.W. 152 Ave.
Goulds, FL 33170
(305)248-0038
Percentage of the business in native species: 100%
Is a catalog or plant list available: No
What is the catalog fee, if any:
Type of business: Retail (x); Wholesale (x); Mail Order
Primary plant focus: Trees & shrubs (x); Herbaceous wildflowers (x);
Grass seed (x); Wildflower seed (x); Cacti or succulents

Environmental Equities, Inc.
12515 Denton Ave.
Hudson, FL 34667
(813)862-3131
Percentage of the business in native species: 95%
Is a catalog or plant list available: Yes
What is the catalog fee, if any: Free
Type of business: Retail (x); Wholesale (x); Mail Order
Primary plant focus: Trees & shrubs (x); Herbaceous wildflowers (x);
Grass seed; Wildflower seed; Cacti or succulents

Farnsworth Farms Nursery
7080 Hypoluxo Farms Road
Lake Worth, FL 33463
(305)965-2657
Percentage of the business in native species: 80%
Is a catalog or plant list available: Yes
What is the catalog fee, if any: N/A
Type of business: Retail (x); Wholesale (x); Mail Order
Primary plant focus: Trees & shrubs (x); Herbaceous wildflowers (x);
Grass seed; Wildflower seed; Cacti or succulents

Florida Division of Forestry
Herren Nursery
1801 SR 70 West
Lake Placid, FL 33852
(813)465-0024
Percentage of the business in native species: 98%
Is a catalog or plant list available: Yes
What is the catalog fee, if any: N/A
Type of business: Retail; Wholesale (x); Mail Order (x)
Primary plant focus: Trees & shrubs (x); Herbaceous wildflowers; Grass
seed; Wildflower seed; Cacti or succulents

Florida Keys Native Nursery, Inc.
102 Mohawk St.
U.S. 1, Mile Marker 89
Tavernier, FL 33070
(305)852-2636
Percentage of the business in native species: 100%
Is a catalog or plant list available: Yes
What is the catalog fee, if any: N/A
Type of business: Retail; Wholesale (x); Mail Order
Primary plant focus: Trees & shrubs (x); Herbaceous wildflowers (x);
Grass seed; Wildflower seed; Cacti or succulents (x)

Florida Scrub Growers
730 Myakka Road
Sarasota, FL 34240
(813)322-1915
Percentage of the business in native species: 95%
Is a catalog or plant list available: Yes
What is the catalog fee, if any: Free
Type of business: Retail (x); Wholesale (x); Mail Order
Primary plant focus: Trees & shrubs (x); Herbaceous wildflowers (x);
Grass seed (x); Wildflower seed; Cacti or succulents

Florida Wildflowers, Inc.
9667 Park Lane
Lake Worth, FL 33467
(407)575-4002
Percentage of the business in native species: 100%
Is a catalog or plant list available: Yes
What is the catalog fee, if any: Free
Type of business: Retail (x); Wholesale (x); Mail Order
Primary plant focus: Trees & shrubs; Herbaceous wildflowers (x); Grass
seed (x); Wildflower seed; Cacti or succulents

Gann's Tropical Greenery & Natives
22140 S. W. 152 Ave.
Goulds, FL 33170
(305)248-5529
Percentage of the business in native species: 100%
Is a catalog or plant list available: Yes
What is the catalog fee, if any: N/A
Type of business: Retail (x); Wholesale (x); Mail Order
Primary plant focus: Trees & shrubs (x); Herbaceous wildflowers (x); Grass seed (x); Wildflower seed; Cacti or succulents

Horticultural Systems, Inc.
P. O. Box 70
Golf Course Road
Parrish, FL 34219
(813)776-1760
Percentage of the business in native species: 100%
Is a catalog or plant list available: Yes
What is the catalog fee, if any: N/A
Type of business: Retail (x); Wholesale (x); Mail Order
Primary plant focus: Trees & shrubs (x); Herbaceous wildflowers (x); Grass seed (x); Wildflower seed (x); Cacti or succulents

Liner Farm
P. O. Box 1369
Saint Cloud, FL 34770-1369
(800)330-1484
Percentage of the business in native species: 12%
Is a catalog or plant list available: Yes
What is the catalog fee, if any: N/A
Type of business: Retail; Wholesale (x); Mail Order
Primary plant focus: Trees & shrubs (x); Herbaceous wildflowers (x); Grass seed; Wildflower seed; Cacti or succulents

Mandarin Native Plants
13500 Mandarin Road
Jacksonville, FL 32223
(904)268-2504
Percentage of the business in native species: 80%
Is a catalog or plant list available: No
What is the catalog fee, if any: Free
Type of business: Retail (x); Wholesale (x); Mail Order
Primary plant focus: Trees & shrubs (x); Herbaceous wildflowers (x);
Grass seed; Wildflower seed; Cacti or succulents

Mesozoic Landscape, Inc.
7667 Park Lane
Lake Worth, FL 33467
(407)967-2630
Percentage of the business in native species: 98%
Is a catalog or plant list available: No
What is the catalog fee, if any:
Type of business: Retail (x); Wholesale (x); Mail Order
Primary plant focus: Trees & shrubs (x); Herbaceous wildflowers; Grass
seed (x); Wildflower seed; Cacti or succulents

Native Green Cay
Rt. 1 Box 331-B
Boynton Beach, FL 33437
(407)496-1415
Percentage of the business in native species: 90%
Is a catalog or plant list available: Yes
What is the catalog fee, if any: N/A
Type of business: Retail; Wholesale (x); Mail Order
Primary plant focus: Trees & shrubs (x); Herbaceous wildflowers; Grass
seed (x); Wildflower seed; Cacti or succulents

Native Nurseries
1661 Centerville Road
Tallahassee, FL 32308
(904)386-8882
Percentage of the business in native species: 80%
Is a catalog or plant list available: Yes
What is the catalog fee, if any: N/A
Type of business: Retail (x); Wholesale; Mail Order
Primary plant focus: Trees & shrubs (x); Herbaceous wildflowers (x); Grass seed; Wildflower seed (x); Cacti or succulents

Native Southeastern Trees, Inc.
P. O. Box 780
Osteen, FL 32764
(407)322-5133
Percentage of the business in native species: 75%
Is a catalog or plant list available: Yes
What is the catalog fee, if any: Free
Type of business: Retail; Wholesale (x); Mail Order
Primary plant focus: Trees & shrubs (x); Herbaceous wildflowers; Grass seed; Wildflower seed; Cacti or succulents

Natives, The
2929 J.B. Carter Road
Davenport, FL 33837
(813)422-6664
Percentage of the business in native species: 100%
Is a catalog or plant list available: Yes
What is the catalog fee, if any: N/A
Type of business: Retail (x); Wholesale (x); Mail Order
Primary plant focus: Trees & shrubs (x); Herbaceous wildflowers (x); Grass seed (x); Wildflower seed; Cacti or succulents

Pine Breeze Nursery
P. O. Box 149
Bokeelia, FL 33922
(813)283-2385
Percentage of the business in native species: 80%
Is a catalog or plant list available: Yes
What is the catalog fee, if any: N/A
Type of business: Retail (x); Wholesale (x); Mail Order
Primary plant focus: Trees & shrubs (x); Herbaceous wildflowers; Grass seed (x); Wildflower seed; Cacti or succulents

Suncoast Native Plants
P. O. Box 248
Palmetto, FL 34220
(813)729-5015
Percentage of the business in native species: 100%
Is a catalog or plant list available: Yes
What is the catalog fee, if any: Free
Type of business: Retail; Wholesale (x); Mail Order
Primary plant focus: Trees & shrubs (x); Herbaceous wildflowers (x); Grass seed (x); Wildflower seed; Cacti or succulents

Superior Trees, Inc.
P. O. Box 9325
Lee, FL 32059
(904)971-5159
Percentage of the business in native species: 95%
Is a catalog or plant list available: Yes
What is the catalog fee, if any: Free
Type of business: Retail; Wholesale (x); Mail Order
Primary plant focus: Trees & shrubs (x); Herbaceous wildflowers; Grass seed; Wildflower seed; Cacti or succulents

The Tree Gallery
8855 116-Terrace S
Boynton Beach, FL 33437
(305)734-4416
Percentage of the business in native species: 100%
Is a catalog or plant list available: Yes
What is the catalog fee, if any: N/A
Type of business: Retail (x); Wholesale (x); Mail Order
Primary plant focus: Trees & shrubs (x); Herbaceous wildflowers; Grass seed; Wildflower seed; Cacti or succulents

The Wetlands Company, Inc.
7650 S. Tamiami Trail, Suite 10
Sarasota, FL 34231
Percentage of the business in native species: 100%
Is a catalog or plant list available: Yes
What is the catalog fee, if any: Free
Type of business: Retail (x); Wholesale (x); Mail Order (x)
Primary plant focus: Trees & shrubs (x); Herbaceous wildflowers (x); Grass seed (x); Wildflower seed; Cacti or succulents

Upland Native Growers of Martin Co.
P. O. Box 855
Palm City, FL 34990
(407)287-2857
Percentage of the business in native species: 100%
Is a catalog or plant list available: Yes
What is the catalog fee, if any: Free
Type of business: Retail; Wholesale (x); Mail Order
Primary plant focus: Trees & shrubs (x); Herbaceous wildflowers (x); Grass seed (x); Wildflower seed; Cacti or succulents (x)

Wetlands Management, Inc.
P. O. Box 1122
Jensen Beach, FL 34958
(407)334-1643
Percentage of the business in native species: 100%
Is a catalog or plant list available: Yes
What is the catalog fee, if any: Free
Type of business: Retail; Wholesale (x); Mail Order
Primary plant focus: Trees & shrubs (x); Herbaceous wildflowers (x); Grass seed (x); Wildflower seed; Cacti or succulents

Wild Azalea Nursery
Route 1 Box 54-B
Brooker, FL 32622
(904)485-1969
Percentage of the business in native species: 95%
Is a catalog or plant list available: Yes
What is the catalog fee, if any: N/A
Type of business: Retail (x); Wholesale; Mail Order
Primary plant focus: Trees & shrubs (x); Herbaceous wildflowers (x); Grass seed (x); Wildflower seed (x); Cacti or succulents (x)

Winding Roads Nursery Corporation
P. O. Box 15905
West Palm Beach, FL 33406
(407)969-1047 or (407)697-3364
Percentage of the business in native species: 85%
Is a catalog or plant list available: N/A
What is the catalog fee, if any:
Type of business: Retail; Wholesale (x); Mail Order
Primary plant focus: Trees & shrubs (x); Herbaceous wildflowers; Grass seed; Wildflower seed; Cacti or succulents

Cedar Lane Farm, Inc.
3790 Sandy Creek Road
Madison, GA 30650
(404)342-2626
Percentage of the business in native species: 40%
Is a catalog or plant list available: Yes
What is the catalog fee, if any: N/A
Type of business: Retail; Wholesale (x); Mail Order
Primary plant focus: Trees & shrubs (x); Herbaceous wildflowers; Grass seed; Wildflower seed; Cacti or succulents

Goodness Grows, Inc.
P. O. Box 576
156 South Woodlawn Dr.
Crawford, GA 30630
(404)743-5055
Percentage of the business in native species: 25%
Is a catalog or plant list available: Yes
What is the catalog fee, if any: N/A
Type of business: Retail (x); Wholesale (x); Mail Order
Primary plant focus: Trees & shrubs (x); Herbaceous wildflowers (x); Grass seed (x); Wildflower seed; Cacti or succulents

Piccadilly Farm
1971 Whippoorwill Road
Bishop, GA 30621
(404)769-6516
Percentage of the business in native species: 15%
Is a catalog or plant list available: Yes
What is the catalog fee, if any: $1.50
Type of business: Retail (x); Wholesale (x); Mail Order (x)
Primary plant focus: Trees & shrubs; Herbaceous wildflowers (x); Grass seed; Wildflower seed; Cacti or succulents

Transplant Nursery
P. O. Box 16
Parkertown Road
Lavonia, GA 30553
(404)356-8947
Percentage of the business in native species: 25%
Is a catalog or plant list available: Yes
What is the catalog fee, if any: N/A
Type of business: Retail (x); Wholesale (x); Mail Order (x)
Primary plant focus: Trees & shrubs; Herbaceous wildflowers (x); Grass seed; Wildflower seed; Cacti or succulents

Twisted Oaks Nursery
P. O. Box 10
Waynesboro, GA 30830
(404)554-3040
Percentage of the business in native species: 40%
Is a catalog or plant list available: Yes
What is the catalog fee, if any: N/A
Type of business: Retail (x); Wholesale (x); Mail Order
Primary plant focus: Trees & shrubs (x); Herbaceous wildflowers; Grass seed; Wildflower seed; Cacti or succulents

Allendan Seed
Rt. 2 Box 31
Winterset, IA 50073
(515)462-1241
Percentage of the business in native species: 100%
Is a catalog or plant list available: Yes
What is the catalog fee, if any: Free
Type of business: Retail (x); Wholesale (x); Mail Order (x)
Primary plant focus: Trees & shrubs; Herbaceous wildflowers; Grass seed (x); Wildflower seed (x); Cacti or succulents

Ion Exchange
Rt. 1 Box 48C
Harpers Ferry, IA 52146
(319)535-7231
Percentage of the business in native species: 95%
Is a catalog or plant list available: Yes
What is the catalog fee, if any: Free
Type of business: Retail (x); Wholesale (x); Mail Order
Primary plant focus: Trees & shrubs (x); Herbaceous wildflowers (x);
Grass seed (x); Wildflower seed (x); Cacti or succulents

Iowa Prairie Seed Co.
Rt. 1 Box 259
Cresco, IA 52136
(319)547-3824
Percentage of the business in native species: 90%
Is a catalog or plant list available: Yes
What is the catalog fee, if any: Free
Type of business: Retail (x); Wholesale (x); Mail Order (x)
Primary plant focus: Trees & shrubs; Herbaceous wildflowers; Grass seed
(x); Wildflower seed (x); Cacti or succulents

Smith Nursery Co.
P. O. Box 515
Charles City, IA 50616
(515)228-3239
Percentage of the business in native species: 25%
Is a catalog or plant list available: Yes
What is the catalog fee, if any: Free
Type of business: Retail (x); Wholesale (x); Mail Order (x)
Primary plant focus: Trees & shrubs (x); Herbaceous wildflowers; Grass
seed; Wildflower seed; Cacti or succulents

Wildflowers From Nature's Way
Rt. 1 Box 62
Woodburn, IA 50275
Percentage of the business in native species: 100%
Is a catalog or plant list available: Yes
What is the catalog fee, if any: $0.50
Type of business: Retail (x); Wholesale; Mail Order (x)
Primary plant focus: Trees & shrubs; Herbaceous wildflowers (x); Grass seed (x); Wildflower seed (x); Cacti or succulents

Fantasy Farms Nursery
P. O. Box 157
Peck, ID 83545
(208)486-6841
Percentage of the business in native species: 75%
Is a catalog or plant list available: Yes
What is the catalog fee, if any: N/A
Type of business: Retail; Wholesale (x); Mail Order (x)
Primary plant focus: Trees & shrubs (x); Herbaceous wildflowers; Grass seed; Wildflower seed; Cacti or succulents

High Altitude Gardens
P. O. Box 4619N
500 Bell Dr. #7
Ketchum, ID 83340
(208)726-3221
Percentage of the business in native species: 80%
Is a catalog or plant list available: Yes
What is the catalog fee, if any: $2.00
Type of business: Retail; Wholesale (x); Mail Order (x)
Primary plant focus: Trees & shrubs; Herbaceous wildflowers (x); Grass seed (x); Wildflower seed (x); Cacti or succulents

Northplan Seed Producer
Silver and Gold Brand Seed
P. O. Box 9107
Moscow, ID 83843
(208)882-8040
Percentage of the business in native species: 90%
Is a catalog or plant list available: Yes
What is the catalog fee, if any: Large SASE
Type of business: Retail; Wholesale; Mail Order (x)
Primary plant focus: Trees & shrubs (x); Herbaceous wildflowers; Grass seed (x); Wildflower seed (x); Cacti or succulents

Winterfeld Ranch Seed (seed farm)
P. O. Box 97
Swan Valley, ID 83449
Percentage of the business in native species: N/A
Is a catalog or plant list available: Yes
What is the catalog fee, if any: N/A
Type of business: Retail; Wholesale; Mail Order
Primary plant focus: Trees & shrubs; Herbaceous wildflowers; Grass seed (x); Wildflower seed (x); Cacti or succulents

Bluestem Prairie Nursery
Rt. 2 Box 106-A
Hillsboro, IL 62049
(217)532-6344
Percentage of the business in native species: 98%
Is a catalog or plant list available: Yes
What is the catalog fee, if any: Free
Type of business: Retail; Wholesale (x); Mail Order (x)
Primary plant focus: Trees & shrubs; Herbaceous wildflowers (x); Grass seed (x); Wildflower seed (x); Cacti or succulents

Country Road Greenhouses, Inc.
Rt. 1 Box 62
Malta, IL 60150
(815)825-2305
Percentage of the business in native species: 100%
Is a catalog or plant list available: Yes
What is the catalog fee, if any: Free
Type of business: Retail; Wholesale (x); Mail Order
Primary plant focus: Trees & shrubs; Herbaceous wildflowers (x); Grass seed; Wildflower seed; Cacti or succulents

Genesis Nursery
Rt. 1 Box 32
Walnut, IL 61376
(815)379-9060
Percentage of the business in native species: 100%
Is a catalog or plant list available: Yes
What is the catalog fee, if any: Free
Type of business: Retail (x); Wholesale (x); Mail Order (x)
Primary plant focus: Trees & shrubs (x); Herbaceous wildflowers (x); Grass seed (x); Wildflower seed (x); Cacti or succulents

Iverson Perennial Gardens, Inc.
P. O. Box 2787 RFD
Long Grove, IL 60047
(708)359-3500
Percentage of the business in native species: Small
Is a catalog or plant list available: Yes
What is the catalog fee, if any: N/A
Type of business: Retail; Wholesale (x); Mail Order
Primary plant focus: Trees & shrubs; Herbaceous wildflowers (x); Grass seed (x); Wildflower seed; Cacti or succulents

LaFayette Home Nursery, Inc.
Rt. 1 Box 1A
LaFayette, IL 61449
(309)995-3311
Percentage of the business in native species: 80%
Is a catalog or plant list available: Yes
What is the catalog fee, if any: $1.00
Type of business: Retail (x); Wholesale (x); Mail Order (x)
Primary plant focus: Trees & shrubs (x); Herbaceous wildflowers (x);
Grass seed (x); Wildflower seed (x); Cacti or succulents

Midwest Wildflowers
P. O. Box 64
Rockton, IL 61072
(815)624-7040
Percentage of the business in native species: 85%
Is a catalog or plant list available: Yes
What is the catalog fee, if any: $1.00
Type of business: Retail (x); Wholesale; Mail Order (x)
Primary plant focus: Trees & shrubs; Herbaceous wildflowers; Grass
seed; Wildflower seed (x); Cacti or succulents

Native Acres
6583 Owen Center Road
Rockford, IL 61101
(815)962-1875
Percentage of the business in native species: 100%
Is a catalog or plant list available: Yes
What is the catalog fee, if any: Free
Type of business: Retail (x); Wholesale (x); Mail Order (x)
Primary plant focus: Trees & shrubs; Herbaceous wildflowers (x); Grass
seed; Wildflower seed; Cacti or succulents

Natural Garden, The
38W443 Highway 64
St. Charles, IL 60175
(312)584-0150
Percentage of the business in native species: 40%
Is a catalog or plant list available: Yes
What is the catalog fee, if any: $2.00
Type of business: Retail (x); Wholesale (x); Mail Order (x)
Primary plant focus: Trees & shrubs; Herbaceous wildflowers (x); Grass seed (x); Wildflower seed (x); Cacti or succulents

Purple Prairie
Rt. 2 Box 176
Wyoming, IL 61491
(309)286-7356
Percentage of the business in native species: 100%
Is a catalog or plant list available: No
What is the catalog fee, if any:
Type of business: Retail; Wholesale (x); Mail Order
Primary plant focus: Trees & shrubs; Herbaceous wildflowers; Grass seed (x); Wildflower seed (x); Cacti or succulents

Sharp Brothers Seed Company
P. O. Box 140
Healy, KS 67850
(316)398-2231
Percentage of the business in native species: 85%
Is a catalog or plant list available: Yes
What is the catalog fee, if any: N/A
Type of business: Retail (x); Wholesale (x); Mail Order (x)
Primary plant focus: Trees & shrubs; Herbaceous wildflowers; Grass seed (x); Wildflower seed (x); Cacti or succulents

Shooting Star Nursery
311 Bates Road
Frankfort, KY 40601
(502)223-1679
Percentage of the business in native species: 100%
Is a catalog or plant list available: Yes
What is the catalog fee, if any: N/A
Type of business: Retail; Wholesale (x); Mail Order (x)
Primary plant focus: Trees & shrubs (x); Herbaceous wildflowers (x); Grass seed (x); Wildflower seed (x); Cacti or succulents

Louisiana Nature and Science Center, Inc.
P. O. Box 870610
New Orleans, LA 70187-0610
Percentage of the business in native species: N/A
Is a catalog or plant list available: N/A
What is the catalog fee, if any:
Type of business: Retail (x); Wholesale; Mail Order (x)
Primary plant focus: Trees & shrubs; Herbaceous wildflowers; Grass seed; Wildflower seed (x); Cacti or succulents

Louisiana Nursery
Rt. 7 Box 43
Opelousas, LA 70570
(318)948-3696
Percentage of the business in native species: N/A
Is a catalog or plant list available: Yes
What is the catalog fee, if any: $5.00
Type of business: Retail (x); Wholesale; Mail Order (x)
Primary plant focus: Trees & shrubs (x); Herbaceous wildflowers (x); Grass seed (x); Wildflower seed; Cacti or succulents

Natives Nurseries
P. O. Box 2355
Old Military Road
Covington, LA 70434
(504)892-5424
Percentage of the business in native species: 80%
Is a catalog or plant list available: Yes
What is the catalog fee, if any: N/A
Type of business: Retail (x); Wholesale (x); Mail Order
Primary plant focus: Trees & shrubs (x); Herbaceous wildflowers; Grass seed; Wildflower seed; Cacti or succulents

Prairie Basse Nursery
Rt. 2 Box 491F
Carencro, LA 70520
(318)896-9187
Percentage of the business in native species: 100%
Is a catalog or plant list available: Yes
What is the catalog fee, if any: SASE
Type of business: Retail (x); Wholesale; Mail Order
Primary plant focus: Trees & shrubs (x); Herbaceous wildflowers (x); Grass seed; Wildflower seed; Cacti or succulents

Donaroma's Nursery
P. O. Box 2189
Upper Main Street
Edgartown, MA 02539
(508)627-8366
Percentage of the business in native species: 20%
Is a catalog or plant list available: Yes
What is the catalog fee, if any: N/A
Type of business: Retail (x); Wholesale; Mail Order
Primary plant focus: Trees & shrubs (x); Herbaceous wildflowers (x); Grass seed (x); Wildflower seed; Cacti or succulents

F. W. Schumacher Co., Inc.
36 Spring Hill Road
Sandwich, MA 02563-1023
(617)888-0659
Percentage of the business in native species: 70%
Is a catalog or plant list available: Yes
What is the catalog fee, if any: N/A
Type of business: Retail (x); Wholesale (x); Mail Order (x)
Primary plant focus: Trees & shrubs (x); Herbaceous wildflowers; Grass seed; Wildflower seed; Cacti or succulents

Rockscapes
Silver Birch Lane
Lincoln, MA 01773
(617)259-8594
Percentage of the business in native species: 50%
Is a catalog or plant list available: Yes
What is the catalog fee, if any: N/A
Type of business: Retail (x); Wholesale (x); Mail Order
Primary plant focus: Trees & shrubs (x); Herbaceous wildflowers (x); Grass seed (x); Wildflower seed; Cacti or succulents

Tripple Brook Farm
37 Middle Road
Southampton, MA 01073
(413)527-4626
Percentage of the business in native species: 25%
Is a catalog or plant list available: Yes
What is the catalog fee, if any: N/A
Type of business: Retail (x); Wholesale (x); Mail Order (x)
Primary plant focus: Trees & shrubs (x); Herbaceous wildflowers (x); Grass seed (x); Wildflower seed; Cacti or succulents (x)

Bluemount Nurseries, Inc.
2103 Blue Mount Road
Monkton, MD 21111
(301)329-6226
Percentage of the business in native species: 10%
Is a catalog or plant list available: Yes
What is the catalog fee, if any: N/A
Type of business: Retail; Wholesale (x); Mail Order
Primary plant focus: Trees & shrubs; Herbaceous wildflowers (x); Grass seed (x); Wildflower seed; Cacti or succulents

Carroll Gardens, Inc.
P. O. Box 310
444 E. Main St.
Westminster, MD 21157
(301)848-5422
Percentage of the business in native species: 2%
Is a catalog or plant list available: Yes
What is the catalog fee, if any: $2.00
Type of business: Retail (x); Wholesale (x); Mail Order (x)
Primary plant focus: Trees & shrubs (x); Herbaceous wildflowers (x); Grass seed; Wildflower seed (x); Cacti or succulents (x)

Crownsville Nursery
P. O. Box 797
Crownsville, MD 21032
(301)923-2212
Percentage of the business in native species: 14%
Is a catalog or plant list available: Yes
What is the catalog fee, if any: $2.00
Type of business: Retail (x); Wholesale; Mail Order (x)
Primary plant focus: Trees & shrubs (x); Herbaceous wildflowers (x); Grass seed (x); Wildflower seed; Cacti or succulents

Environmental Concern, Inc.
P. O. Box P
210 W. Chew Ave.
St. Michaels, MD 21663
(301)745-9620
Percentage of the business in native species: 50%
Is a catalog or plant list available: N/A
What is the catalog fee, if any:
Type of business: Retail (x); Wholesale (x); Mail Order (x)
Primary plant focus: Trees & shrubs (x); Herbaceous wildflowers (x); Grass seed (x); Wildflower seed (x); Cacti or succulents

Kurt Bluemel, Inc.
2740 Greene Lane
Baldwin, MD 21013
(301)557-7229
Percentage of the business in native species: 15%
Is a catalog or plant list available: Yes
What is the catalog fee, if any: $2.00
Type of business: Retail (x); Wholesale (x); Mail Order (x)
Primary plant focus: Trees & shrubs; Herbaceous wildflowers (x); Grass seed (x); Wildflower seed; Cacti or succulents

Native Seeds, Inc.
14590 Tridelphia Mill Road
Dayton, MD 21036
(301)596-9818
Percentage of the business in native species: 100%
Is a catalog or plant list available: Yes
What is the catalog fee, if any: N/A
Type of business: Retail (x); Wholesale (x); Mail Order (x)
Primary plant focus: Trees & shrubs; Herbaceous wildflowers; Grass seed; Wildflower seed (x); Cacti or succulents

Sylva Native Nursery & Seed Co.
1927 York Road
Timonium, MD 21093
(301)560-2288
Percentage of the business in native species: 100%
Is a catalog or plant list available: Yes
What is the catalog fee, if any: N/A
Type of business: Retail; Wholesale (x); Mail Order
Primary plant focus: Trees & shrubs (x); Herbaceous wildflowers (x); Grass seed (x); Wildflower seed (x); Cacti or succulents

Sylva Native Nursery & Seed Co.
21221 Mikules Manner Lane
Freeland, MD 21053
(301)560-2288
Percentage of the business in native species: 100%
Is a catalog or plant list available: Yes
What is the catalog fee, if any: N/A
Type of business: Retail; Wholesale (x); Mail Order
Primary plant focus: Trees & shrubs (x); Herbaceous wildflowers (x); Grass seed (x); Wildflower seed (x); Cacti or succulents

Wildflower
6 Oaklyn Ct.
Potomac, MD 20854-3933
(301)983-2607
Percentage of the business in native species: 66%
Is a catalog or plant list available: Yes
What is the catalog fee, if any: $0.50 postage
Type of business: Retail (x); Wholesale (x); Mail Order
Primary plant focus: Trees & shrubs (x); Herbaceous wildflowers (x); Grass seed; Wildflower seed; Cacti or succulents

Armintrout's West Michigan Farms, Inc.
1156 Lincoln Road
Allegan, MI 49010
(616)673-6627
Percentage of the business in native species: Small
Is a catalog or plant list available: Yes
What is the catalog fee, if any: Free
Type of business: Retail; Wholesale (x); Mail Order
Primary plant focus: Trees & shrubs (x); Herbaceous wildflowers; Grass seed; Wildflower seed; Cacti or succulents

Hortech
P. O. Box 16
Spring Lake, MI 49456
(616)842-1392
Percentage of the business in native species: 10%
Is a catalog or plant list available: Yes
What is the catalog fee, if any: Free
Type of business: Retail; Wholesale (x); Mail Order
Primary plant focus: Trees & shrubs (x); Herbaceous wildflowers (x); Grass seed; Wildflower seed; Cacti or succulents

Kalamazoo Wildflower Nursery
922 Grant
Kalamazoo, MI 49008
(616)342-4910
Percentage of the business in native species: 100%
Is a catalog or plant list available: No
What is the catalog fee, if any:
Type of business: Retail (x); Wholesale; Mail Order
Primary plant focus: Trees & shrubs; Herbaceous wildflowers (x); Grass seed; Wildflower seed (x); Cacti or succulents

Michigan Wildflower Farm, The
11770 Cutler Road
Portland, MI 48875-9452
(517)647-6010
Percentage of the business in native species: 100%
Is a catalog or plant list available: Yes
What is the catalog fee, if any: Free
Type of business: Retail (x); Wholesale (x); Mail Order (x)
Primary plant focus: Trees & shrubs; Herbaceous wildflowers (x); Grass seed; Wildflower seed (x); Cacti or succulents

Oikos Tree Crops
721 N. Fletcher
Kalamazoo, MI 49007-3077
(616)342-6504
Percentage of the business in native species: 15%
Is a catalog or plant list available: Yes
What is the catalog fee, if any: Free
Type of business: Retail (x); Wholesale (x); Mail Order (x)
Primary plant focus: Trees & shrubs (x); Herbaceous wildflowers; Grass seed; Wildflower seed; Cacti or succulents

Vans Pines Nursery
7550 144th Ave. W
Mt. Olive, MI 49460
(616)399-1620
Percentage of the business in native species: Small
Is a catalog or plant list available: Yes
What is the catalog fee, if any: Free
Type of business: Retail (x); Wholesale (x); Mail Order (x)
Primary plant focus: Trees & shrubs (x); Herbaceous wildflowers; Grass seed; Wildflower seed; Cacti or succulents

Wavecrest Nursery
2509 Lakeshore Dr.
Fennville, MI 49408
(616)543-4175
Percentage of the business in native species: Small
Is a catalog or plant list available: Yes
What is the catalog fee, if any: $1.00
Type of business: Retail (x); Wholesale (x); Mail Order (x)
Primary plant focus: Trees & shrubs (x); Herbaceous wildflowers; Grass seed; Wildflower seed; Cacti or succulents

Wildside, The
4815 Valley Ave.
Hudsonville, MI 49426
(616)669-3256
Percentage of the business in native species: 98%
Is a catalog or plant list available: Yes
What is the catalog fee, if any: SASE
Type of business: Retail; Wholesale (x); Mail Order (x)
Primary plant focus: Trees & shrubs; Herbaceous wildflowers (x); Grass seed (x); Wildflower seed (x); Cacti or succulents

Bailey Nurseries, Inc.
1325 Bailey Road
St. Paul, MN 55119
(612)459-9744
Percentage of the business in native species: Small
Is a catalog or plant list available: Yes
What is the catalog fee, if any: N/A
Type of business: Retail; Wholesale (x); Mail Order
Primary plant focus: Trees & shrubs (x); Herbaceous wildflowers; Grass seed; Wildflower seed; Cacti or succulents

Feder's Prairie Seed Co.
Rt. 1 Box 41
Blue Earth, MN 56013
(507)526-3049
Percentage of the business in native species: 100%
Is a catalog or plant list available: Yes
What is the catalog fee, if any: Free
Type of business: Retail (x); Wholesale (x); Mail Order (x)
Primary plant focus: Trees & shrubs; Herbaceous wildflowers; Grass seed (x); Wildflower seed (x); Cacti or succulents

Landscape Alternatives, Inc.
1465 N. Pascal St.
St. Paul, MN 55108
(612)488-3142
Percentage of the business in native species: 97%
Is a catalog or plant list available: Yes
What is the catalog fee, if any: $1.00
Type of business: Retail (x); Wholesale (x); Mail Order (x)
Primary plant focus: Trees & shrubs; Herbaceous wildflowers (x); Grass seed (x); Wildflower seed (x); Cacti or succulents

Mohn Frontier Seed and Nursery
Rt. 1 Box 152
Cottonwood, MN 56229
(507)423-6482
Percentage of the business in native species: 75%
Is a catalog or plant list available: Yes
What is the catalog fee, if any: Free
Type of business: Retail (x); Wholesale (x); Mail Order
Primary plant focus: Trees & shrubs; Herbaceous wildflowers; Grass seed (x); Wildflower seed (x); Cacti or succulents

Orchid Gardens
2232 139th Ave. NW
Andover, MN 55304
(612)755-0205
Percentage of the business in native species: 95%
Is a catalog or plant list available: Yes
What is the catalog fee, if any: $0.75
Type of business: Retail (x); Wholesale; Mail Order (x)
Primary plant focus: Trees & shrubs (x); Herbaceous wildflowers (x);
Grass seed; Wildflower seed; Cacti or succulents

Prairie Hill Wildflowers
Rt. 1 Box 191-A
Ellendale, MN 56026
(507)451-7791
Percentage of the business in native species: 100%
Is a catalog or plant list available: Yes
What is the catalog fee, if any: N/A
Type of business: Retail (x); Wholesale (x); Mail Order
Primary plant focus: Trees & shrubs (x); Herbaceous wildflowers (x);
Grass seed (x); Wildflower seed (x); Cacti or succulents

Prairie Moon Nursery
Rt. 1 Box 163
Winona, MN 55987
(507)452-1362
Percentage of the business in native species: 99%
Is a catalog or plant list available: Yes
What is the catalog fee, if any: $2.00
Type of business: Retail (x); Wholesale (x); Mail Order (x)
Primary plant focus: Trees & shrubs; Herbaceous wildflowers (x); Grass
seed (x); Wildflower seed (x); Cacti or succulents

Prairie Restorations, Inc.
P. O. Box 327
Princeton, MN 55371
(612)389-4342
Percentage of the business in native species: 100%
Is a catalog or plant list available: Yes
What is the catalog fee, if any: Free
Type of business: Retail (x); Wholesale (x); Mail Order (x)
Primary plant focus: Trees & shrubs (x); Herbaceous wildflowers (x); Grass seed (x); Wildflower seed (x); Cacti or succulents

Rice Creek Gardens, Inc.
11506 Highway 65
Blaine, MN 55434
(612)754-8090
Percentage of the business in native species: Small
Is a catalog or plant list available: Yes
What is the catalog fee, if any: $2.00
Type of business: Retail (x); Wholesale (x); Mail Order (x)
Primary plant focus: Trees & shrubs (x); Herbaceous wildflowers (x); Grass seed; Wildflower seed; Cacti or succulents (x)

S & R Seed Dealers, Inc.
P. O. Box 1087
Cass Lake, MN 56633
(218)335-2363
Percentage of the business in native species: 100%
Is a catalog or plant list available: Yes
What is the catalog fee, if any: Free
Type of business: Retail (x); Wholesale (x); Mail Order (x)
Primary plant focus: Trees & shrubs (x); Herbaceous wildflowers; Grass seed; Wildflower seed; Cacti or succulents

Shady Acres Herb Farm
7815 Highway 212
Chaska, MN 55318
(612)466-3391
Percentage of the business in native species: Small
Is a catalog or plant list available: Yes
What is the catalog fee, if any: N/A
Type of business: Retail (x); Wholesale; Mail Order
Primary plant focus: Trees & shrubs; Herbaceous wildflowers (x); Grass seed; Wildflower seed; Cacti or succulents

Elixir Farm Botanicals
General Delivery
Brixey, MO 65618
(417)261-2393
Percentage of the business in native species: 50%
Is a catalog or plant list available: Yes
What is the catalog fee, if any: $2.00
Type of business: Retail (x); Wholesale; Mail Order (x)
Primary plant focus: Trees & shrubs; Herbaceous wildflowers (x); Grass seed; Wildflower seed (x); Cacti or succulents

Forrest Keeling Nursery
P. O. Box 135
Elsberry, MO 63343
(800)332-3361
Percentage of the business in native species: 20%
Is a catalog or plant list available: Yes
What is the catalog fee, if any: Free
Type of business: Retail; Wholesale (x); Mail Order
Primary plant focus: Trees & shrubs (x); Herbaceous wildflowers; Grass seed; Wildflower seed; Cacti or succulents

Hamilton Seeds and Wildflowers

HCR 9 Box 138
Elk Creek, MO 65464
(417)967-2190

Percentage of the business in native species: 97%
Is a catalog or plant list available: Yes
What is the catalog fee, if any: Free
Type of business: Retail (x); Wholesale (x); Mail Order (x)
Primary plant focus: Trees & shrubs (x); Herbaceous wildflowers (x); Grass seed (x); Wildflower seed (x); Cacti or succulents

J & J Seeds

Rt. 3
Gallatin, MO 64640
(816)663-3190

Percentage of the business in native species: 75%
Is a catalog or plant list available: Yes
What is the catalog fee, if any: N/A
Type of business: Retail (x); Wholesale (x); Mail Order
Primary plant focus: Trees & shrubs; Herbaceous wildflowers; Grass seed (x); Wildflower seed; Cacti or succulents

Missouri Wildflowers Nursery

Rt. 2 Box 373
9814 Pleasant Hill Road
Jefferson City, MO 65109
(314)496-3492

Percentage of the business in native species: 100%
Is a catalog or plant list available: Yes
What is the catalog fee, if any: $1.00
Type of business: Retail (x); Wholesale (x); Mail Order (x)
Primary plant focus: Trees & shrubs; Herbaceous wildflowers (x); Grass seed (x); Wildflower seed (x); Cacti or succulents

Sharp Brothers Seed Company
Rt. 4 Box 237A
Clinton, MO 64735
(816)885-7551
Percentage of the business in native species: 80%
Is a catalog or plant list available: Yes
What is the catalog fee, if any: $1.00
Type of business: Retail (x); Wholesale (x); Mail Order (x)
Primary plant focus: Trees & shrubs; Herbaceous wildflowers; Grass seed (x); Wildflower seed (x); Cacti or succulents

Homochitto Outdoors
P. O. Box 630
#3 Franklin St.
Meadville, MS 39653
(601)384-2915
Percentage of the business in native species: 92%
Is a catalog or plant list available: Yes
What is the catalog fee, if any: $1.00
Type of business: Retail (x); Wholesale (x); Mail Order (x)
Primary plant focus: Trees & shrubs; Herbaceous wildflowers; Grass seed; Wildflower seed (x); Cacti or succulents

Bitterroot Native Growers, Inc.
P. O. Box 566
Hamilton, MT 59840
(406)961-4702
Percentage of the business in native species: 100%
Is a catalog or plant list available: Yes
What is the catalog fee, if any: N/A
Type of business: Retail; Wholesale (x); Mail Order (x)
Primary plant focus: Trees & shrubs (x); Herbaceous wildflowers (x); Grass seed (x); Wildflower seed; Cacti or succulents

Lawyer Nursery, Inc.
950 Highway 200 W
Plains, MT 59859
(406)826-3881
Percentage of the business in native species: 30%
Is a catalog or plant list available: Yes
What is the catalog fee, if any: Free
Type of business: Retail; Wholesale (x); Mail Order (x)
Primary plant focus: Trees & shrubs (x); Herbaceous wildflowers; Grass seed; Wildflower seed; Cacti or succulents

Valley Nursery
P. O. Box 4845
Helena, MT 59604
Percentage of the business in native species: 50%
Is a catalog or plant list available: Yes
What is the catalog fee, if any: $0.30
Type of business: Retail (x); Wholesale (x); Mail Order (x)
Primary plant focus: Trees & shrubs (x); Herbaceous wildflowers (x); Grass seed; Wildflower seed; Cacti or succulents

Wild Flower Seeds
Ruth Unger
16100 Highway 10-A W
Anaconda, MT 59711
(406)563-8048
Percentage of the business in native species: 100%
Is a catalog or plant list available: Yes
What is the catalog fee, if any: $1.00
Type of business: Retail (x); Wholesale (x); Mail Order (x)
Primary plant focus: Trees & shrubs (x); Herbaceous wildflowers; Grass seed (x); Wildflower seed (x); Cacti or succulents

A Source for SEED & Special PLANTS
Rt. 68 Box 301
Tuckasegee, NC 28783
(704)293-5206
Percentage of the business in native species: 100%
Is a catalog or plant list available: Yes
What is the catalog fee, if any: $1.00
Type of business: Retail (x); Wholesale (x); Mail Order (x)
Primary plant focus: Trees & shrubs (x); Herbaceous wildflowers (x); Grass seed (x); Wildflower seed (x); Cacti or succulents

Boothe Hill Tea Company and Greenhouse
23-B Boothe Hill
Chapel Hill, NC 27514
(919)967-4091
Percentage of the business in native species: 85%
Is a catalog or plant list available: Yes
What is the catalog fee, if any: N/A
Type of business: Retail; Wholesale (x); Mail Order (x)
Primary plant focus: Trees & shrubs; Herbaceous wildflowers (x); Grass seed; Wildflower seed (x); Cacti or succulents

Brookside Wildflowers
Rt. 3 Box 740
Boone, NC 28607
(704)963-5548
Percentage of the business in native species: 95%
Is a catalog or plant list available: Yes
What is the catalog fee, if any: $2.00
Type of business: Retail (x); Wholesale (x); Mail Order (x)
Primary plant focus: Trees & shrubs; Herbaceous wildflowers (x); Grass seed; Wildflower seed; Cacti or succulents

Carolina Seacoast Beachgrass
P. O. Box 1194
Morehead City, NC 28557
(919)240-2415
Percentage of the business in native species: 100%
Is a catalog or plant list available: Yes
What is the catalog fee, if any: N/A
Type of business: Retail (x); Wholesale (x); Mail Order (x)
Primary plant focus: Trees & shrubs; Herbaceous wildflowers; Grass seed (x); Wildflower seed; Cacti or succulents

Gardens of the Blue Ridge
P. O. Box 10
Pineola, NC 28662
(704)733-2417
Percentage of the business in native species: 100%
Is a catalog or plant list available: Yes
What is the catalog fee, if any: $2.00
Type of business: Retail (x); Wholesale (x); Mail Order (x)
Primary plant focus: Trees & shrubs (x); Herbaceous wildflowers (x); Grass seed; Wildflower seed (x); Cacti or succulents

Holbrook Farm & Nursery
Rt. 2 Box 223B
Fletcher, NC 28732
(704)891-7790
Percentage of the business in native species: N/A
Is a catalog or plant list available: Yes
What is the catalog fee, if any: $2.00
Type of business: Retail (x); Wholesale; Mail Order (x)
Primary plant focus: Trees & shrubs; Herbaceous wildflowers (x); Grass seed; Wildflower seed; Cacti or succulents

Humphries Nursery
Rt. 7 Box 202C
Durham, NC 27707
(919)489-0952
Percentage of the business in native species: 30%
Is a catalog or plant list available: Yes
What is the catalog fee, if any: SASE
Type of business: Retail (x); Wholesale (x); Mail Order
Primary plant focus: Trees & shrubs; Herbaceous wildflowers (x); Grass seed; Wildflower seed; Cacti or succulents

Hungry Plants
1216 Cooper Dr.
Raleigh, NC 27607
(919)829-3751
Percentage of the business in native species: 30%
Is a catalog or plant list available: Yes
What is the catalog fee, if any: $1.00
Type of business: Retail (x); Wholesale (x); Mail Order (x)
Primary plant focus: Trees & shrubs; Herbaceous wildflowers; Grass seed; Wildflower seed; Cacti or succulents

Lamtree Farm
Rt. 1 Box 162
Warrensville, NC 28693
(919)385-6144
Percentage of the business in native species: 95%
Is a catalog or plant list available: Yes
What is the catalog fee, if any: $1.00
Type of business: Retail (x); Wholesale (x); Mail Order (x)
Primary plant focus: Trees & shrubs (x); Herbaceous wildflowers; Grass seed; Wildflower seed; Cacti or succulents

Montrose Nursery
P. O. Box 957
Hillsborough, NC 27278
(919)732-7787
Percentage of the business in native species: 30%
Is a catalog or plant list available: Yes
What is the catalog fee, if any: $2.00
Type of business: Retail (x); Wholesale; Mail Order (x)
Primary plant focus: Trees & shrubs; Herbaceous wildflowers (x); Grass seed; Wildflower seed; Cacti or succulents

Moser Growers
Rt. 1 Box 269
Whittier, NC 28789
(704)497-7118
Percentage of the business in native species: 40%
Is a catalog or plant list available: Yes
What is the catalog fee, if any: N/A
Type of business: Retail; Wholesale (x); Mail Order
Primary plant focus: Trees & shrubs (x); Herbaceous wildflowers; Grass seed; Wildflower seed; Cacti or succulents

Niche Gardens
1111 Dawson Road
Chapel Hill, NC 27516-8576
(919)967-0078
Percentage of the business in native species: 90%
Is a catalog or plant list available: Yes
What is the catalog fee, if any: $3.00
Type of business: Retail (x); Wholesale; Mail Order (x)
Primary plant focus: Trees & shrubs (x); Herbaceous wildflowers (x); Grass seed (x); Wildflower seed; Cacti or succulents (x)

Take Root (specializing in ferns)
4 Blakes Dr.
Pittsboro, NC 27312
(919)967-9515
Percentage of the business in native species: 90%
Is a catalog or plant list available: Yes
What is the catalog fee, if any: N/A
Type of business: Retail; Wholesale (x); Mail Order (x)
Primary plant focus: Trees & shrubs; Herbaceous wildflowers (x); Grass seed; Wildflower seed; Cacti or succulents

We-Du Nurseries
Rt. 5 Box 724
Marion, NC 28752
(704)738-8300
Percentage of the business in native species: 90%
Is a catalog or plant list available: Yes
What is the catalog fee, if any: $1.00
Type of business: Retail (x); Wholesale; Mail Order (x)
Primary plant focus: Trees & shrubs (x); Herbaceous wildflowers (x); Grass seed (x); Wildflower seed; Cacti or succulents

Aurora McTurf
P. O. Box 194
Aurora, NE 68818
(308)381-7092
Percentage of the business in native species: 100%
Is a catalog or plant list available: Yes
What is the catalog fee, if any: N/A
Type of business: Retail (x); Wholesale (x); Mail Order (x)
Primary plant focus: Trees & shrubs; Herbaceous wildflowers; Grass seed (x); Wildflower seed; Cacti or succulents

Bluebird Nursery, Inc.
P. O. Box 460
Clarkson, NE 68629
(402)892-3457
Percentage of the business in native species: 40%
Is a catalog or plant list available: Yes
What is the catalog fee, if any: N/A
Type of business: Retail (x); Wholesale (x); Mail Order
Primary plant focus: Trees & shrubs (x); Herbaceous wildflowers (x); Grass seed; Wildflower seed; Cacti or succulents

Flatland Impressions
1307 L St.
Aurora, NE 68818
(402)694-5535
Percentage of the business in native species: 100%
Is a catalog or plant list available: No
What is the catalog fee, if any:
Type of business: Retail (x); Wholesale (x); Mail Order
Primary plant focus: Trees & shrubs; Herbaceous wildflowers (x); Grass seed; Wildflower seed; Cacti or succulents

Paul E. Allen Farm Supply
Rt. 2 Box 8
Bristow, NE 68719-9407
(402)583-9924
Percentage of the business in native species: 100%
Is a catalog or plant list available: Yes
What is the catalog fee, if any: N/A
Type of business: Retail (x); Wholesale (x); Mail Order (x)
Primary plant focus: Trees & shrubs; Herbaceous wildflowers; Grass seed; Wildflower seed (x); Cacti or succulents

Stock Seed Farms, Inc.
Rt. 1 Box 112
Murdock, NE 68407
(402)867-3771
Percentage of the business in native species: 90%
Is a catalog or plant list available: Yes
What is the catalog fee, if any: Free
Type of business: Retail (x); Wholesale (x); Mail Order (x)
Primary plant focus: Trees & shrubs; Herbaceous wildflowers (x); Grass seed (x); Wildflower seed (x); Cacti or succulents

Jonathan Green, Inc.
P. O. Box 326
Farmingdale, NJ 07727
(201)938-7007
Percentage of the business in native species: 10%
Is a catalog or plant list available: No
What is the catalog fee, if any:
Type of business: Retail; Wholesale (x); Mail Order
Primary plant focus: Trees & shrubs; Herbaceous wildflowers; Grass seed (x); Wildflower seed (x); Cacti or succulents

Loft Seed, Inc.
Chimney Rock Road
Bound Brook, NJ 08805
(201)560-1590
Percentage of the business in native species: 50%
Is a catalog or plant list available: Yes
What is the catalog fee, if any: N/A
Type of business: Retail (x); Wholesale (x); Mail Order (x)
Primary plant focus: Trees & shrubs; Herbaceous wildflowers; Grass seed (x); Wildflower seed (x); Cacti or succulents

Wild Earth Native Plant Nursery
49 Mead Ave.
Freehold, NJ 07728
(908)780-5661
Percentage of the business in native species: 95%
Is a catalog or plant list available: Yes
What is the catalog fee, if any: N/A
Type of business: Retail (x); Wholesale (x); Mail Order
Primary plant focus: Trees & shrubs; Herbaceous wildflowers (x); Grass seed; Wildflower seed; Cacti or succulents

Agua Fria Nursery, Inc.
1709 Agua Fria
Santa Fe, NM 87501
(505)983-4831
Percentage of the business in native species: 34%
Is a catalog or plant list available: No
What is the catalog fee, if any:
Type of business: Retail (x); Wholesale; Mail Order
Primary plant focus: Trees & shrubs (x); Herbaceous wildflowers (x); Grass seed (x); Wildflower seed; Cacti or succulents

Bernardo Beach Native Plant Farm
1 Sanchez Road
Veguita, NM 87062
(505)345-6248
Percentage of the business in native species: 80%
Is a catalog or plant list available: Yes
What is the catalog fee, if any: Four first class stamps
Type of business: Retail (x); Wholesale; Mail Order (x)
Primary plant focus: Trees & shrubs (x); Herbaceous wildflowers (x); Grass seed (x); Wildflower seed (x); Cacti or succulents (x)

C. H. & E. Diebold, Ltd.
268 La Ladera Road
Los Lunas, NM 87031
(515)869-2517
Percentage of the business in native species: 90%
Is a catalog or plant list available: No
What is the catalog fee, if any:
Type of business: Retail; Wholesale (x); Mail Order
Primary plant focus: Trees & shrubs; Herbaceous wildflowers (x); Grass seed (x); Wildflower seed; Cacti or succulents

Curtis and Curtis Seed and Supply, Inc.
Star Route Box 8-A
Clovis, NM 88101
(505)762-4759
Percentage of the business in native species: 80%
Is a catalog or plant list available: No
What is the catalog fee, if any:
Type of business: Retail (x); Wholesale (x); Mail Order (x)
Primary plant focus: Trees & shrubs (x); Herbaceous wildflowers (x); Grass seed (x); Wildflower seed (x); Cacti or succulents

Desert Moon Nursery
P. O. Box 600
Veguita, NM 87062
(505)864-0614
Percentage of the business in native species: 90%
Is a catalog or plant list available: Yes
What is the catalog fee, if any: $1.00
Type of business: Retail (x); Wholesale (x); Mail Order (x)
Primary plant focus: Trees & shrubs (x); Herbaceous wildflowers (x); Grass seed; Wildflower seed; Cacti or succulents (x)

H & H Wholesale Nursery, Inc.
P. O. Box 1078
Las Cruces, NM 88004
(505)524-2571
Percentage of the business in native species: 50%
Is a catalog or plant list available: Yes
What is the catalog fee, if any: Free
Type of business: Retail; Wholesale (x); Mail Order
Primary plant focus: Trees & shrubs (x); Herbaceous wildflowers (x); Grass seed (x); Wildflower seed; Cacti or succulents (x)

Mesa Garden
P. O. Box 72
Belen, NM 87002-0072
(505)864-3131
Percentage of the business in native species: 20%
Is a catalog or plant list available: Yes
What is the catalog fee, if any: Two first class stamps
Type of business: Retail (x); Wholesale; Mail Order (x)
Primary plant focus: Trees & shrubs; Herbaceous wildflowers; Grass seed; Wildflower seed; Cacti or succulents (x)

New Mexico Cactus Research
P. O. Box 787, Dept. 135
1132 East River Road
Belen, NM 87002
(505)864-4027
Percentage of the business in native species: 10%
Is a catalog or plant list available: Yes
What is the catalog fee, if any: SASE
Type of business: Retail (x); Wholesale (x); Mail Order (x)
Primary plant focus: Trees & shrubs; Herbaceous wildflowers; Grass seed; Wildflower seed; Cacti or succulents (x)

Plants of the Southwest
930 Baca St.
Santa Fe, NM 87501
(505)983-1548
Percentage of the business in native species: 90%
Is a catalog or plant list available: Yes
What is the catalog fee, if any: $1.50
Type of business: Retail (x); Wholesale (x); Mail Order (x)
Primary plant focus: Trees & shrubs (x); Herbaceous wildflowers (x);
Grass seed (x); Wildflower seed (x); Cacti or succulents

Seed Futures
P. O. Box 2010
Sparks, NV 89432
Percentage of the business in native species: 100%
Is a catalog or plant list available: Yes
What is the catalog fee, if any: N/A
Type of business: Retail (x); Wholesale (x); Mail Order (x)
Primary plant focus: Trees & shrubs (x); Herbaceous wildflowers (x);
Grass seed (x); Wildflower seed (x); Cacti or succulents

Panfield Nursery
322 Southdown Road
Huntington, NY 11743
(516)427-0112
Percentage of the business in native species: 80%
Is a catalog or plant list available: Yes
What is the catalog fee, if any: N/A
Type of business: Retail (x); Wholesale (x); Mail Order
Primary plant focus: Trees & shrubs (x); Herbaceous wildflowers (x);
Grass seed (x); Wildflower seed; Cacti or succulents

Stanford Seed-Bentley Division
P. O. Box 38
Cambridge, NY 12812
(800)327-6155
Percentage of the business in native species: N/A
Is a catalog or plant list available: No
What is the catalog fee, if any:
Type of business: Retail; Wholesale; Mail Order
Primary plant focus: Trees & shrubs; Herbaceous wildflowers; Grass seed; Wildflower seed (x); Cacti or succulents

Wildginger Woodlands
P. O. Box 1091
Webster, NY 14580
Percentage of the business in native species: 95%
Is a catalog or plant list available: Yes
What is the catalog fee, if any: $1.00
Type of business: Retail (x); Wholesale; Mail Order (x)
Primary plant focus: Trees & shrubs; Herbaceous wildflowers (x); Grass seed; Wildflower seed (x); Cacti or succulents

Garden Place
P. O. Box 388
6780 Heisley Road
Mentor, OH 44061-0388
(216)255-3705
Percentage of the business in native species: N/A
Is a catalog or plant list available: Yes
What is the catalog fee, if any: $1.00
Type of business: Retail (x); Wholesale (x); Mail Order (x)
Primary plant focus: Trees & shrubs; Herbaceous wildflowers (x); Grass seed (x); Wildflower seed; Cacti or succulents

Valley Creek, Inc.
P. O. Box 475
Circle Drive
McArthur, OH 45651
(615)596-2521
Percentage of the business in native species: 100%
Is a catalog or plant list available: Yes
What is the catalog fee, if any: N/A
Type of business: Retail (x); Wholesale (x); Mail Order (x)
Primary plant focus: Trees & shrubs; Herbaceous wildflowers; Grass seed; Wildflower seed (x); Cacti or succulents

Guy's Seed Co.
2520 Main
Woodward, OK 73801
(405)254-2926
Percentage of the business in native species: 90%
Is a catalog or plant list available: Yes
What is the catalog fee, if any: $1.50
Type of business: Retail (x); Wholesale (x); Mail Order
Primary plant focus: Trees & shrubs; Herbaceous wildflowers; Grass seed (x); Wildflower seed (x); Cacti or succulents

Jenco Wholesale Nurseries, Inc.
P. O. Box 752
4902 East 121 St. South
Bixby, OK 74008-0752
(918)369-2091
Percentage of the business in native species: 5%
Is a catalog or plant list available: Yes
What is the catalog fee, if any: N/A
Type of business: Retail; Wholesale (x); Mail Order
Primary plant focus: Trees & shrubs (x); Herbaceous wildflowers (x); Grass seed (x); Wildflower seed (x); Cacti or succulents

Johnston Seed Company
P. O. Box 1392
Enid, OK 73702
(405)233-5800
Percentage of the business in native species: 30%
Is a catalog or plant list available: Yes
What is the catalog fee, if any: N/A
Type of business: Retail (x); Wholesale (x); Mail Order (x)
Primary plant focus: Trees & shrubs; Herbaceous wildflowers; Grass seed (x); Wildflower seed (x); Cacti or succulents

Callahan Seeds
6045 Foley Lane
Central Point, OR 97502
(503)855-1164
Percentage of the business in native species: 90%
Is a catalog or plant list available: Yes
What is the catalog fee, if any: SASE
Type of business: Retail (x); Wholesale (x); Mail Order (x)
Primary plant focus: Trees & shrubs (x); Herbaceous wildflowers; Grass seed; Wildflower seed; Cacti or succulents

Forestfarm
990 Tetherwild Road
Williams, OR 97544
(503)846-6963
Percentage of the business in native species: 40%
Is a catalog or plant list available: Yes
What is the catalog fee, if any: $2.00
Type of business: Retail; Wholesale; Mail Order (x)
Primary plant focus: Trees & shrubs (x); Herbaceous wildflowers (x); Grass seed (x); Wildflower seed; Cacti or succulents

Great Western Seed Company
P. O. Box 387
810 Jackson St. SE
Albany, OR 97321
(503)928-3100
Percentage of the business in native species: N/A
Is a catalog or plant list available: Yes
What is the catalog fee, if any: N/A
Type of business: Retail; Wholesale (x); Mail Order
Primary plant focus: Trees & shrubs; Herbaceous wildflowers; Grass seed (x); Wildflower seed (x); Cacti or succulents

Greer Gardens
1280 Goodpasture Island Road
Eugene, OR 97401
(503)686-8266
Percentage of the business in native species: N/A
Is a catalog or plant list available: Yes
What is the catalog fee, if any: $3.00
Type of business: Retail (x); Wholesale; Mail Order (x)
Primary plant focus: Trees & shrubs (x); Herbaceous wildflowers; Grass seed (x); Wildflower seed; Cacti or succulents

Russell Graham
Purveyor of Plants
4030 Eagle Crest Road NW
Salem, OR 97304
(503)362-1135
Percentage of the business in native species: 40%
Is a catalog or plant list available: Yes
What is the catalog fee, if any: $2.00
Type of business: Retail (x); Wholesale (x); Mail Order (x)
Primary plant focus: Trees & shrubs; Herbaceous wildflowers (x); Grass seed; Wildflower seed; Cacti or succulents

Siskiyou Rare Plant Nursery
2825 Cummings Road
Medford, OR 97501
(503)772-6846
Percentage of the business in native species: N/A
Is a catalog or plant list available: Yes
What is the catalog fee, if any: $2.00
Type of business: Retail (x); Wholesale; Mail Order (x)
Primary plant focus: Trees & shrubs (x); Herbaceous wildflowers (x);
Grass seed; Wildflower seed; Cacti or succulents

Turf Seed, Inc.
3017 G St.
Hubbard, OR 97032
(503)981-9571
Percentage of the business in native species: 10%
Is a catalog or plant list available: Yes
What is the catalog fee, if any: N/A
Type of business: Retail; Wholesale (x); Mail Order
Primary plant focus: Trees & shrubs; Herbaceous wildflowers; Grass seed
(x); Wildflower seed (x); Cacti or succulents

Appalachian Wildflower Nursery
Rt. 1 Box 275A
Reedsville, PA 17084
(717)667-6998
Percentage of the business in native species: 50%
Is a catalog or plant list available: Yes
What is the catalog fee, if any: $1.25
Type of business: Retail (x); Wholesale; Mail Order (x)
Primary plant focus: Trees & shrubs (x); Herbaceous wildflowers (x);
Grass seed; Wildflower seed; Cacti or succulents

Carino Nurseries
P. O. Box 538
Indiana, PA 15701
(800)223-7075
Percentage of the business in native species: 20%
Is a catalog or plant list available: Yes
What is the catalog fee, if any: N/A
Type of business: Retail (x); Wholesale (x); Mail Order (x)
Primary plant focus: Trees & shrubs (x); Herbaceous wildflowers; Grass seed; Wildflower seed; Cacti or succulents

England's Herb Farm
Rt. 1 Box 706
Todd and White School House roads
Honey Brook, PA 19344
(215)273-2863
Percentage of the business in native species: 40%
Is a catalog or plant list available: Yes
What is the catalog fee, if any: $2.00
Type of business: Retail (x); Wholesale (x); Mail Order (x)
Primary plant focus: Trees & shrubs; Herbaceous wildflowers (x); Grass seed; Wildflower seed; Cacti or succulents

Johnston Nurseries
Rt. 1 Box 100
Creekside, PA 15732
(412)463-8456
Percentage of the business in native species: 10%
Is a catalog or plant list available: Yes
What is the catalog fee, if any: N/A
Type of business: Retail; Wholesale (x); Mail Order (x)
Primary plant focus: Trees & shrubs (x); Herbaceous wildflowers; Grass seed; Wildflower seed; Cacti or succulents

Natural Landscapes
354 N. Jennersville Road
West Grove, PA 19390
(215)869-3788
Percentage of the business in native species: 95%
Is a catalog or plant list available: Yes
What is the catalog fee, if any: N/A
Type of business: Retail; Wholesale (x); Mail Order
Primary plant focus: Trees & shrubs (x); Herbaceous wildflowers (x);
Grass seed; Wildflower seed; Cacti or succulents

Primrose Path, The
Rt. 2 Box 110
Scottdale, PA 15683
(412)887-6756
Percentage of the business in native species: 50%
Is a catalog or plant list available: Yes
What is the catalog fee, if any: $2.00
Type of business: Retail (x); Wholesale; Mail Order (x)
Primary plant focus: Trees & shrubs; Herbaceous wildflowers (x); Grass
seed; Wildflower seed; Cacti or succulents

W. Atlee Burpee Co.
300 Park Ave.
Warminster, PA 18974
(215)674-4900
Percentage of the business in native species: N/A
Is a catalog or plant list available: Yes
What is the catalog fee, if any: N/A
Type of business: Retail; Wholesale (x); Mail Order (x)
Primary plant focus: Trees & shrubs (x); Herbaceous wildflowers (x);
Grass seed (x); Wildflower seed (x); Cacti or succulents

Wildflower Patch
442 RC Brookside
Walnutport, PA 18088
(215)767-3195
Percentage of the business in native species: 80%
Is a catalog or plant list available: Yes
What is the catalog fee, if any: $1.00
Type of business: Retail (x); Wholesale; Mail Order (x)
Primary plant focus: Trees & shrubs; Herbaceous wildflowers; Grass seed; Wildflower seed (x); Cacti or succulents

Oak Hill Farm
204 Pressly St.
Clover, SC 29710-1233
(803)222-4245
Percentage of the business in native species: 90%
Is a catalog or plant list available: Yes
What is the catalog fee, if any: N/A
Type of business: Retail (x); Wholesale (x); Mail Order (x)
Primary plant focus: Trees & shrubs (x); Herbaceous wildflowers; Grass seed; Wildflower seed; Cacti or succulents

Tom Dodd Nurseries-Carolina
5500 Dorchester Road
North Charleston, SC 29418
(803)767-2932
Percentage of the business in native species: 50%
Is a catalog or plant list available: Yes
What is the catalog fee, if any: N/A
Type of business: Retail (x); Wholesale (x); Mail Order
Primary plant focus: Trees & shrubs (x); Herbaceous wildflowers; Grass seed; Wildflower seed; Cacti or succulents

Woodlanders, Inc.
1128 Colleton Ave.
Aiken, SC 29801
(803)648-7522
Percentage of the business in native species: 60%
Is a catalog or plant list available: Yes
What is the catalog fee, if any: 3-ounce postage
Type of business: Retail (x); Wholesale; Mail Order (x)
Primary plant focus: Trees & shrubs (x); Herbaceous wildflowers (x);
Grass seed (x); Wildflower seed; Cacti or succulents (x)

Northern Plains Seed Co.
P. O. Box 964
Sioux Falls, SD 57101
(605)336-0623
Percentage of the business in native species: 15%
Is a catalog or plant list available: No
What is the catalog fee, if any:
Type of business: Retail (x); Wholesale (x); Mail Order
Primary plant focus: Trees & shrubs; Herbaceous wildflowers; Grass seed
(x); Wildflower seed (x); Cacti or succulents

Rethke Nursery
P. O. Box 82
Milbank, SD 57252
(605)432-6073
Percentage of the business in native species: 40%
Is a catalog or plant list available: Yes
What is the catalog fee, if any: Free
Type of business: Retail; Wholesale (x); Mail Order
Primary plant focus: Trees & shrubs (x); Herbaceous wildflowers; Grass
seed (x); Wildflower seed; Cacti or succulents

Herbert Nature Center
373 Cedar Branch Road
Kingsport, TN 37664
(615)323-9601
Percentage of the business in native species: 99%
Is a catalog or plant list available: Yes
What is the catalog fee, if any: Free
Type of business: Retail (x); Wholesale; Mail Order
Primary plant focus: Trees & shrubs; Herbaceous wildflowers (x); Grass seed; Wildflower seed; Cacti or succulents

Native Gardens
Columbine Farm
Rt. 1 Box 494
Greenback, TN 37742
(615)856-3350
Percentage of the business in native species: 99%
Is a catalog or plant list available: Yes
What is the catalog fee, if any: $1.00
Type of business: Retail (x); Wholesale (x); Mail Order (x)
Primary plant focus: Trees & shrubs (x); Herbaceous wildflowers (x); Grass seed (x); Wildflower seed (x); Cacti or succulents

Sunlight Gardens, Inc.
Rt. 1 Box 600A
Andersonville, TN 37705
(615)494-8237
Percentage of the business in native species: 95%
Is a catalog or plant list available: Yes
What is the catalog fee, if any: $2.00
Type of business: Retail (x); Wholesale (x); Mail Order (x)
Primary plant focus: Trees & shrubs (x); Herbaceous wildflowers (x); Grass seed; Wildflower seed (x); Cacti or succulents

Aldridge Nursery, Inc.
P. O. Box 1299
Van Ormy, TX 78073
(512)622-3491
Percentage of the business in native species: 10%
Is a catalog or plant list available: No
What is the catalog fee, if any:
Type of business: Retail; Wholesale (x); Mail Order
Primary plant focus: Trees & shrubs (x); Herbaceous wildflowers; Grass seed; Wildflower seed; Cacti or succulents

Anderson Landscape and Nursery
2222 Peck
Houston, TX 77055
(713)984-1342
Percentage of the business in native species: 75%
Is a catalog or plant list available: Yes
What is the catalog fee, if any: N/A
Type of business: Retail (x); Wholesale (x); Mail Order
Primary plant focus: Trees & shrubs (x); Herbaceous wildflowers (x); Grass seed; Wildflower seed; Cacti or succulents

Annis Nursery
5180 Highway 290 W
Austin, TX 78735
(512)892-5280
Percentage of the business in native species: 20%
Is a catalog or plant list available: No
What is the catalog fee, if any:
Type of business: Retail (x); Wholesale; Mail Order
Primary plant focus: Trees & shrubs (x); Herbaceous wildflowers (x); Grass seed (x); Wildflower seed (x); Cacti or succulents (x)

Antique Rose Emporium, The
Rt. 5 Box 143
Brenham, TX 77833
(409)836-9051
Percentage of the business in native species: 20%
Is a catalog or plant list available: Yes
What is the catalog fee, if any: $3.00
Type of business: Retail (x); Wholesale (x); Mail Order (x)
Primary plant focus: Trees & shrubs (x); Herbaceous wildflowers (x);
Grass seed (x); Wildflower seed; Cacti or succulents

Bamert Seed Co.
Rt. 3 Box 1120
Muleshoe, TX 79347
(806)272-4787
Percentage of the business in native species: 100%
Is a catalog or plant list available: Yes
What is the catalog fee, if any: N/A
Type of business: Retail (x); Wholesale (x); Mail Order
Primary plant focus: Trees & shrubs; Herbaceous wildflowers; Grass seed
(x); Wildflower seed; Cacti or succulents

Barton Springs Nursery
3601 Bee Caves Rd.
Austin, TX 78746
(512)328-6655
Percentage of the business in native species: 60%
Is a catalog or plant list available: No
What is the catalog fee, if any:
Type of business: Retail (x); Wholesale; Mail Order
Primary plant focus: Trees & shrubs (x); Herbaceous wildflowers (x);
Grass seed (x); Wildflower seed (x); Cacti or succulents (x)

Breed & Co.
718 W. 29th St.
Austin, TX 78705
(512)474-7058
Percentage of the business in native species: 25%
Is a catalog or plant list available: No
What is the catalog fee, if any:
Type of business: Retail (x); Wholesale; Mail Order
Primary plant focus: Trees & shrubs (x); Herbaceous wildflowers (x); Grass seed; Wildflower seed (x); Cacti or succulents

Browning Seed, Inc.
P. O. Box 1836
South IH 27
Plainview, TX 79073-1836
(806)293-5271
Percentage of the business in native species: 10%
Is a catalog or plant list available: No
What is the catalog fee, if any:
Type of business: Retail; Wholesale (x); Mail Order
Primary plant focus: Trees & shrubs; Herbaceous wildflowers; Grass seed (x); Wildflower seed; Cacti or succulents

Buchanan's Native Plants
111 Heights Blvd.
Houston, TX 77007
(713)861-5702
Percentage of the business in native species: 30%
Is a catalog or plant list available: No
What is the catalog fee, if any:
Type of business: Retail (x); Wholesale; Mail Order
Primary plant focus: Trees & shrubs (x); Herbaceous wildflowers (x); Grass seed (x); Wildflower seed (x); Cacti or succulents

Buck's Sod and Sales, Inc.
P. O. Box 906
Sweeny, TX 77480
(409)548-3776
Percentage of the business in native species: 100%
Is a catalog or plant list available: No
What is the catalog fee, if any:
Type of business: Retail; Wholesale (x); Mail Order
Primary plant focus: Trees & shrubs (x); Herbaceous wildflowers; Grass seed (x); Wildflower seed; Cacti or succulents

Cactus Farm, The
Rt. 5 Box 1610
Nacogdoches, TX 75961
(409)560-6406
Percentage of the business in native species: 30%
Is a catalog or plant list available: Yes
What is the catalog fee, if any: N/A
Type of business: Retail; Wholesale (x); Mail Order (x)
Primary plant focus: Trees & shrubs; Herbaceous wildflowers; Grass seed; Wildflower seed; Cacti or succulents (x)

Callahan's General Store
501 Bastrop Highway
Austin, TX 78741
(512)385-3452
Percentage of the business in native species: N/A
Is a catalog or plant list available: No
What is the catalog fee, if any:
Type of business: Retail (x); Wholesale (x); Mail Order
Primary plant focus: Trees & shrubs; Herbaceous wildflowers; Grass seed (x); Wildflower seed (x); Cacti or succulents

Chaparral Estates Gardens
Rt. 1 Box 425
Killeen, TX 76542
(817)526-3973
Percentage of the business in native species: 50%
Is a catalog or plant list available: No
What is the catalog fee, if any:
Type of business: Retail (x); Wholesale (x); Mail Order
Primary plant focus: Trees & shrubs (x); Herbaceous wildflowers (x);
Grass seed; Wildflower seed; Cacti or succulents

Compleat Gardens, The
5405 Broadway
San Antonio, TX 78209
(512)822-0444
Percentage of the business in native species: 10%
Is a catalog or plant list available: No
What is the catalog fee, if any:
Type of business: Retail (x); Wholesale; Mail Order
Primary plant focus: Trees & shrubs (x); Herbaceous wildflowers (x);
Grass seed (x); Wildflower seed (x); Cacti or succulents (x)

Conlee Seed Company, Inc.
P. O. Box 23219
481 Texas Central Parkway
Waco, TX 76702-3219
(817)772-5680
Percentage of the business in native species: N/A
Is a catalog or plant list available: Yes
What is the catalog fee, if any: N/A
Type of business: Retail; Wholesale (x); Mail Order
Primary plant focus: Trees & shrubs; Herbaceous wildflowers; Grass seed
(x); Wildflower seed (x); Cacti or succulents

Cook Seed Company
P. O. Box 33185
3206 Locke Lane
Austin, TX 78764
(512)441-2889
Percentage of the business in native species: 100%
Is a catalog or plant list available: Yes
What is the catalog fee, if any: Free
Type of business: Retail; Wholesale; Mail Order (x)
Primary plant focus: Trees & shrubs; Herbaceous wildflowers; Grass seed (x); Wildflower seed (x); Cacti or succulents

Dodds Family Tree
515 W. Main
Fredericksburg, TX 78624
(512)997-9571
Percentage of the business in native species: 20%
Is a catalog or plant list available: No
What is the catalog fee, if any:
Type of business: Retail (x); Wholesale; Mail Order
Primary plant focus: Trees & shrubs (x); Herbaceous wildflowers; Grass seed; Wildflower seed (x); Cacti or succulents (x)

Douglass W. King Co., Inc.
P. O. Box 200320
San Antonio, TX 78220
(512)661-4191
Percentage of the business in native species: 30%
Is a catalog or plant list available: Yes
What is the catalog fee, if any: $2.95
Type of business: Retail (x); Wholesale (x); Mail Order (x)
Primary plant focus: Trees & shrubs; Herbaceous wildflowers; Grass seed (x); Wildflower seed (x); Cacti or succulents

Foster Rambie Grass Seed
326 N. Second St.
Garner Field
Uvalde, TX 78801
(512)278-2711
Percentage of the business in native species: 50%
Is a catalog or plant list available: N/A
What is the catalog fee, if any:
Type of business: Retail (x); Wholesale (x); Mail Order (x)
Primary plant focus: Trees & shrubs; Herbaceous wildflowers; Grass seed (x); Wildflower seed (x); Cacti or succulents

Freda's Forest Nursery
3020 N. Francis Ave.
Odessa, TX 79764
(915)381-3517
Percentage of the business in native species: 95%
Is a catalog or plant list available: Yes
What is the catalog fee, if any: SASE
Type of business: Retail (x); Wholesale (x); Mail Order (x)
Primary plant focus: Trees & shrubs (x); Herbaceous wildflowers (x); Grass seed (x); Wildflower seed (x); Cacti or succulents (x)

Gardens
1818 W. 35th St.
Austin, TX 78703
(512)451-5490
Percentage of the business in native species: 30%
Is a catalog or plant list available: No
What is the catalog fee, if any:
Type of business: Retail (x); Wholesale; Mail Order
Primary plant focus: Trees & shrubs (x); Herbaceous wildflowers (x); Grass seed (x); Wildflower seed (x); Cacti or succulents (x)

Garrison Seed Company
P. O. Drawer 2420
East Highway 60
Hereford, TX 79045
(806)364-0560
Percentage of the business in native species: 15%
Is a catalog or plant list available: Yes
What is the catalog fee, if any: N/A
Type of business: Retail (x); Wholesale (x); Mail Order
Primary plant focus: Trees & shrubs; Herbaceous wildflowers; Grass seed (x); Wildflower seed (x); Cacti or succulents

George Warner Seed Co.
P. O. Box 1448
Hereford, TX 79045
(806)364-4470
Percentage of the business in native species: 10%
Is a catalog or plant list available: Yes
What is the catalog fee, if any: N/A
Type of business: Retail (x); Wholesale (x); Mail Order
Primary plant focus: Trees & shrubs; Herbaceous wildflowers; Grass seed (x); Wildflower seed; Cacti or succulents

Gone Native Nursery
1407 E. County Rd. 130
Midland, TX 79701
(915)686-9632
Percentage of the business in native species: 90%
Is a catalog or plant list available: No
What is the catalog fee, if any:
Type of business: Retail (x); Wholesale; Mail Order
Primary plant focus: Trees & shrubs (x); Herbaceous wildflowers (x); Grass seed; Wildflower seed; Cacti or succulents

Green Horizons
218 Quinlan #571
Kerrville, TX 78028
(512)257-5141
Percentage of the business in native species: 100%
Is a catalog or plant list available: Yes
What is the catalog fee, if any: SASE
Type of business: Retail (x); Wholesale; Mail Order (x)
Primary plant focus: Trees & shrubs; Herbaceous wildflowers; Grass seed (x); Wildflower seed (x); Cacti or succulents

Green 'n Growing
P. O. Box 855
601 West Pecan
Pflugerville, TX 78660
(512)251-3262
Percentage of the business in native species: 10%
Is a catalog or plant list available: No
What is the catalog fee, if any:
Type of business: Retail (x); Wholesale; Mail Order
Primary plant focus: Trees & shrubs (x); Herbaceous wildflowers (x); Grass seed (x); Wildflower seed (x); Cacti or succulents

Greenhouse Nursery, The
4402 W. University Dr.
McKinney, TX 75070
(214)548-9122
Percentage of the business in native species: 20%
Is a catalog or plant list available: Yes
What is the catalog fee, if any: N/A
Type of business: Retail (x); Wholesale; Mail Order
Primary plant focus: Trees & shrubs (x); Herbaceous wildflowers (x); Grass seed (x); Wildflower seed (x); Cacti or succulents (x)

Gunsight Mountain Ranch and Nursery
P. O. Box 86
Tarpley, TX 78883
(512)562-3225
Percentage of the business in native species: 98%
Is a catalog or plant list available: Yes
What is the catalog fee, if any: Free
Type of business: Retail (x); Wholesale (x); Mail Order
Primary plant focus: Trees & shrubs (x); Herbaceous wildflowers (x);
Grass seed; Wildflower seed; Cacti or succulents

Harpool Farm and Garden
420 E. McKinney
Denton, TX 76201
(817)387-0541
Percentage of the business in native species: 50%
Is a catalog or plant list available: No
What is the catalog fee, if any:
Type of business: Retail (x); Wholesale; Mail Order
Primary plant focus: Trees & shrubs (x); Herbaceous wildflowers (x);
Grass seed (x); Wildflower seed (x); Cacti or succulents (x)

Hill Country Landscape Garden Center
P. O. Box 201297
11603 Jollyville Road
Austin, TX 78720
(512)258-0093
Percentage of the business in native species: 30%
Is a catalog or plant list available: No
What is the catalog fee, if any:
Type of business: Retail (x); Wholesale; Mail Order
Primary plant focus: Trees & shrubs (x); Herbaceous wildflowers (x);
Grass seed (x); Wildflower seed (x); Cacti or succulents (x)

Island Botanics (contract growers only)
(native coastal wetland vegetation)
714 Don Patricio
Corpus Christi, TX 78418
Percentage of the business in native species: 100%
Is a catalog or plant list available: Yes
What is the catalog fee, if any: N/A
Type of business: Retail; Wholesale; Mail Order
Primary plant focus: Trees & shrubs (x); Herbaceous wildflowers; Grass
seed (x); Wildflower seed; Cacti or succulents

J'Don Seeds International
P. O. Box 10998-533
Austin, TX 78766
(512)343-6360
Percentage of the business in native species: 95%
Is a catalog or plant list available: Yes
What is the catalog fee, if any: N/A
Type of business: Retail; Wholesale (x); Mail Order (x)
Primary plant focus: Trees & shrubs; Herbaceous wildflowers; Grass
seed; Wildflower seed (x); Cacti or succulents

Jenco Wholesale Nurseries
P. O. Box 200755
4601 Switch Willo Road
Austin, TX 78720-0755
(512)346-0562
Percentage of the business in native species: 25%
Is a catalog or plant list available: Yes
What is the catalog fee, if any: N/A
Type of business: Retail; Wholesale (x); Mail Order
Primary plant focus: Trees & shrubs (x); Herbaceous wildflowers; Grass
seed; Wildflower seed (x); Cacti or succulents

Jenco Wholesale Nurseries, Inc.
P. O. Box 6
1611 N. I-35, Suite 410
Carrollton, TX 75006-3814
(214)446-1820
Percentage of the business in native species: 5%
Is a catalog or plant list available: Yes
What is the catalog fee, if any: N/A
Type of business: Retail; Wholesale (x); Mail Order
Primary plant focus: Trees & shrubs (x); Herbaceous wildflowers (x);
Grass seed (x); Wildflower seed (x); Cacti or succulents

Jenco Wholesale Nurseries, Inc.
P. O. Box 16625
1211 Alcove Ave.
Lubbock, TX 79490
(806)799-3646
Percentage of the business in native species: 5%
Is a catalog or plant list available: Yes
What is the catalog fee, if any: N/A
Type of business: Retail; Wholesale (x); Mail Order
Primary plant focus: Trees & shrubs (x); Herbaceous wildflowers (x);
Grass seed (x); Wildflower seed (x); Cacti or succulents

Jenco Wholesale Nurseries, Inc.
P. O. Box 292336
1120 S. Texas
Lewisville, TX 75029-2336
(214)219-1509
Percentage of the business in native species: 5%
Is a catalog or plant list available: Yes
What is the catalog fee, if any: N/A
Type of business: Retail; Wholesale (x); Mail Order
Primary plant focus: Trees & shrubs (x); Herbaceous wildflowers (x);
Grass seed (x); Wildflower seed (x); Cacti or succulents

Kings Creek Gardens
813 Straus Road
Cedar Hill, TX 75104
(214)291-7650
Percentage of the business in native species: 80%
Is a catalog or plant list available: Yes
What is the catalog fee, if any: N/A
Type of business: Retail (x); Wholesale; Mail Order
Primary plant focus: Trees & shrubs (x); Herbaceous wildflowers (x);
Grass seed (x); Wildflower seed (x); Cacti or succulents

Lone Star Growers
Rt. 9 Box 220
7960 Cagnon Road
San Antonio, TX 78227
(512)677-8020
Percentage of the business in native species: 20%
Is a catalog or plant list available: Yes
What is the catalog fee, if any: N/A
Type of business: Retail; Wholesale (x); Mail Order
Primary plant focus: Trees & shrubs (x); Herbaceous wildflowers (x);
Grass seed (x); Wildflower seed; Cacti or succulents

Lowrey Nursery, The
2323 Sleepy Hollow Road
Conroe, TX 77385
(713)367-4076
Percentage of the business in native species: 85%
Is a catalog or plant list available: N/A
What is the catalog fee, if any:
Type of business: Retail (x); Wholesale; Mail Order (x)
Primary plant focus: Trees & shrubs (x); Herbaceous wildflowers (x);
Grass seed (x); Wildflower seed (x); Cacti or succulents

Madrone Nursery
Rt. 2 Box 12
San Marcos, TX 78666
(512)353-3944
Percentage of the business in native species: 95%
Is a catalog or plant list available: Yes
What is the catalog fee, if any: N/A
Type of business: Retail (x); Wholesale (x); Mail Order
Primary plant focus: Trees & shrubs (x); Herbaceous wildflowers (x);
Grass seed (x); Wildflower seed; Cacti or succulents

Miller Grass Seed Company
P. O. Box 886
Hereford, TX 79045
(806)258-7288
Percentage of the business in native species: 70%
Is a catalog or plant list available: Yes
What is the catalog fee, if any: N/A
Type of business: Retail (x); Wholesale (x); Mail Order
Primary plant focus: Trees & shrubs; Herbaceous wildflowers; Grass seed
(x); Wildflower seed (x); Cacti or succulents

Native American Seed
2088 W. Jeter Road
Argyle, TX 76226
(214)539-0534
Percentage of the business in native species: 100%
Is a catalog or plant list available: Yes
What is the catalog fee, if any: $1.00
Type of business: Retail; Wholesale; Mail Order (x)
Primary plant focus: Trees & shrubs; Herbaceous wildflowers; Grass seed
(x); Wildflower seed (x); Cacti or succulents

Native Ornamentals
P. O. Box 997
Mertzon, TX 76941
(915)835-2021
Percentage of the business in native species: 100%
Is a catalog or plant list available: Yes
What is the catalog fee, if any: $1.00
Type of business: Retail (x); Wholesale; Mail Order
Primary plant focus: Trees & shrubs (x); Herbaceous wildflowers; Grass seed; Wildflower seed (x); Cacti or succulents (x)

Native Son Plant Nursery
507 Lockhart Dr.
Austin, TX 78704
(512)444-2610
Percentage of the business in native species: 99%
Is a catalog or plant list available: Yes
What is the catalog fee, if any: N/A
Type of business: Retail (x); Wholesale (x); Mail Order
Primary plant focus: Trees & shrubs (x); Herbaceous wildflowers (x); Grass seed (x); Wildflower seed (x); Cacti or succulents

Native Texas Nursery
1007 MoPac Circle, Suite 101
Austin, TX 78746
(512)328-2004
Percentage of the business in native species: 95%
Is a catalog or plant list available: Yes
What is the catalog fee, if any: N/A
Type of business: Retail; Wholesale (x); Mail Order
Primary plant focus: Trees & shrubs (x); Herbaceous wildflowers (x); Grass seed (x); Wildflower seed; Cacti or succulents

Native Tree Farm
3302 Primrose
Georgetown, TX 78628
(512)863-6268
Percentage of the business in native species: 90%
Is a catalog or plant list available: Yes
What is the catalog fee, if any: N/A
Type of business: Retail (x); Wholesale (x); Mail Order
Primary plant focus: Trees & shrubs (x); Herbaceous wildflowers; Grass seed; Wildflower seed; Cacti or succulents

Oak Hill Native Plant Nursery
792 Oakdale Dr.
Austin, TX 78745
(512)892-0690
Percentage of the business in native species: 98%
Is a catalog or plant list available: No
What is the catalog fee, if any:
Type of business: Retail (x); Wholesale; Mail Order
Primary plant focus: Trees & shrubs (x); Herbaceous wildflowers (x); Grass seed (x); Wildflower seed; Cacti or succulents

Powers Wholesale Nursery
7310 Sherwood Road
Austin, TX 78745
(512)444-5511
Percentage of the business in native species: 20%
Is a catalog or plant list available: Yes
What is the catalog fee, if any: N/A
Type of business: Retail; Wholesale (x); Mail Order
Primary plant focus: Trees & shrubs (x); Herbaceous wildflowers (x); Grass seed (x); Wildflower seed (x); Cacti or succulents

Proseed (U.S.A.), Inc.
P. O. Box 1250
1800 IH-35 S
San Marcos, TX 78667
(512)392-1900
Percentage of the business in native species: N/A
Is a catalog or plant list available: No
What is the catalog fee, if any:
Type of business: Retail; Wholesale (x); Mail Order
Primary plant focus: Trees & shrubs; Herbaceous wildflowers; Grass seed (x); Wildflower seed (x); Cacti or succulents

Red Barn Nurseries
Rt. 3 Box 445
Elgin, TX 78621
(512)335-0122
Percentage of the business in native species: 65%
Is a catalog or plant list available: No
What is the catalog fee, if any:
Type of business: Retail (x); Wholesale; Mail Order
Primary plant focus: Trees & shrubs (x); Herbaceous wildflowers (x); Grass seed (x); Wildflower seed (x); Cacti or succulents (x)

Robinson Seed Co.
1113 Jefferson Dr.
Plainview, TX 79072
(806)293-4959
Percentage of the business in native species: 100%
Is a catalog or plant list available: No
What is the catalog fee, if any:
Type of business: Retail (x); Wholesale (x); Mail Order (x)
Primary plant focus: Trees & shrubs; Herbaceous wildflowers; Grass seed (x); Wildflower seed (x); Cacti or succulents

Samadhi Farms
Rt. 2 Box 173
Bastrop, TX 78602
(512)285-2661
Percentage of the business in native species: 100%
Is a catalog or plant list available: Yes
What is the catalog fee, if any: Free
Type of business: Retail; Wholesale (x); Mail Order
Primary plant focus: Trees & shrubs (x); Herbaceous wildflowers (x);
Grass seed; Wildflower seed; Cacti or succulents

Scherz Landscape Co.
P. O. Box 60087
2225 Knickerbock Road
San Angelo, TX 76906
(915)944-0511
Percentage of the business in native species: 50%
Is a catalog or plant list available: No
What is the catalog fee, if any:
Type of business: Retail (x); Wholesale (x); Mail Order
Primary plant focus: Trees & shrubs (x); Herbaceous wildflowers; Grass
seed; Wildflower seed; Cacti or succulents

Shades of Green
334 W. Sunset Road
San Antonio, TX 78209
(512)824-3772
Percentage of the business in native species: 30%
Is a catalog or plant list available: No
What is the catalog fee, if any:
Type of business: Retail (x); Wholesale; Mail Order
Primary plant focus: Trees & shrubs (x); Herbaceous wildflowers (x);
Grass seed; Wildflower seed (x); Cacti or succulents

Sharp Brothers Seed Company
Rt. 9 Box 2
8700 Dumas Dr.
Amarillo, TX 79108
(806)383-7772
Percentage of the business in native species: 75%
Is a catalog or plant list available: Yes
What is the catalog fee, if any: N/A
Type of business: Retail (x); Wholesale (x); Mail Order (x)
Primary plant focus: Trees & shrubs; Herbaceous wildflowers; Grass seed (x); Wildflower seed; Cacti or succulents

Spring Creek Nursery
HC 66 Box 240
Mertzon, TX 76941
(915)835-3203
Percentage of the business in native species: 100%
Is a catalog or plant list available: Yes
What is the catalog fee, if any: N/A
Type of business: Retail (x); Wholesale (x); Mail Order
Primary plant focus: Trees & shrubs (x); Herbaceous wildflowers (x); Grass seed (x); Wildflower seed (x); Cacti or succulents (x)

Storm Nursery, Inc.
P. O. Box 889
Premont, TX 78375
(512)348-3521
Percentage of the business in native species: N/A
Is a catalog or plant list available: Yes
What is the catalog fee, if any: N/A
Type of business: Retail (x); Wholesale (x); Mail Order
Primary plant focus: Trees & shrubs (x); Herbaceous wildflowers; Grass seed; Wildflower seed; Cacti or succulents

Sunbelt Trees, Inc.
16008 Boss Gaston
Richmond, TX 77469
(800)635-4313
Percentage of the business in native species: 15%
Is a catalog or plant list available: Yes
What is the catalog fee, if any: N/A
Type of business: Retail; Wholesale (x); Mail Order
Primary plant focus: Trees & shrubs (x); Herbaceous wildflowers; Grass seed; Wildflower seed; Cacti or succulents

Texas Native Trees
P. O. Box 817
Leander, TX 78641
(512)259-3006
Percentage of the business in native species: 95%
Is a catalog or plant list available: Yes
What is the catalog fee, if any: N/A
Type of business: Retail; Wholesale (x); Mail Order (x)
Primary plant focus: Trees & shrubs (x); Herbaceous wildflowers (x); Grass seed (x); Wildflower seed (x); Cacti or succulents

Texas Seed Co., Inc.
P. O. Drawer 599
221 Airport Blvd.
Kenedy, TX 78119
(512)583-9873
Percentage of the business in native species: 5%
Is a catalog or plant list available: Yes
What is the catalog fee, if any: N/A
Type of business: Retail (x); Wholesale (x); Mail Order (x)
Primary plant focus: Trees & shrubs; Herbaceous wildflowers; Grass seed (x); Wildflower seed (x); Cacti or succulents

Texas Star Gardens
P. O. Box 663
Abilene, TX 79604
(915)692-2733
Percentage of the business in native species: 98%
Is a catalog or plant list available: Yes
What is the catalog fee, if any: N/A
Type of business: Retail; Wholesale (x); Mail Order
Primary plant focus: Trees & shrubs (x); Herbaceous wildflowers (x); Grass seed (x); Wildflower seed; Cacti or succulents

Turner Seed Company, Inc.
Rt. 1 Box 292
Breckenridge, TX 76024
(817)559-2065
Percentage of the business in native species: 30%
Is a catalog or plant list available: Yes
What is the catalog fee, if any: N/A
Type of business: Retail (x); Wholesale; Mail Order (x)
Primary plant focus: Trees & shrubs; Herbaceous wildflowers (x); Grass seed (x); Wildflower seed (x); Cacti or succulents

W. H. Anton Seed Co., Inc.
P. O. Box 667
Lockhart, TX 78644
(512)398-2433
Percentage of the business in native species: 5%
Is a catalog or plant list available: Yes
What is the catalog fee, if any: N/A
Type of business: Retail (x); Wholesale (x); Mail Order
Primary plant focus: Trees & shrubs; Herbaceous wildflowers; Grass seed (x); Wildflower seed; Cacti or succulents

Weston Gardens in Bloom, Inc.
8101 Anglin Dr.
Fort Worth, TX 76140
(817)572-0549
Percentage of the business in native species: 90%
Is a catalog or plant list available: Yes
What is the catalog fee, if any: N/A
Type of business: Retail (x); Wholesale; Mail Order
Primary plant focus: Trees & shrubs (x); Herbaceous wildflowers (x);
Grass seed (x); Wildflower seed (x); Cacti or succulents

Wildseed, Inc.
P. O. Box 308
1101 Campo Rosa Road
Eagle Lake, TX 77434
(409)234-7353
Percentage of the business in native species: 90%
Is a catalog or plant list available: Yes
What is the catalog fee, if any: N/A
Type of business: Retail (x); Wholesale (x); Mail Order (x)
Primary plant focus: Trees & shrubs; Herbaceous wildflowers (x); Grass
seed (x); Wildflower seed (x); Cacti or succulents

Granite Seed Company
P. O. Box 177
Lehi, UT 84043
(801)768-4422
Percentage of the business in native species: 80%
Is a catalog or plant list available: Yes
What is the catalog fee, if any: $2.50
Type of business: Retail; Wholesale (x); Mail Order
Primary plant focus: Trees & shrubs (x); Herbaceous wildflowers (x);
Grass seed (x); Wildflower seed (x); Cacti or succulents

Intermountain Cactus
2344 South Redwood Road
Salt Lake City, UT 84119
(801)972-5149
Percentage of the business in native species: 100%
Is a catalog or plant list available: Yes
What is the catalog fee, if any: One first-class stamp
Type of business: Retail (x); Wholesale; Mail Order (x)
Primary plant focus: Trees & shrubs; Herbaceous wildflowers; Grass seed; Wildflower seed; Cacti or succulents (x)

Stevenson Intermountain Seed
P. O. Box 2
488 S. 100 East
Ephraim, UT 84627
(801)283-6639
Percentage of the business in native species: 80%
Is a catalog or plant list available: Yes
What is the catalog fee, if any: Free
Type of business: Retail (x); Wholesale (x); Mail Order
Primary plant focus: Trees & shrubs (x); Herbaceous wildflowers (x); Grass seed (x); Wildflower seed (x); Cacti or succulents

Virginia Natives
Wildside Farm
P. O. Box 18
Hume, VA 22639
(703)364-1001
Percentage of the business in native species: 99%
Is a catalog or plant list available: Yes
What is the catalog fee, if any: $1.00
Type of business: Retail (x); Wholesale (x); Mail Order
Primary plant focus: Trees & shrubs; Herbaceous wildflowers (x); Grass seed (x); Wildflower seed; Cacti or succulents (x)

Virginia Wilde Farms
Rt. 2 Box 1512
Hanover, VA 23069
(804)643-0021
Percentage of the business in native species: 85%
Is a catalog or plant list available: Yes
What is the catalog fee, if any: $2.00
Type of business: Retail (x); Wholesale (x); Mail Order (x)
Primary plant focus: Trees & shrubs (x); Herbaceous wildflowers (x);
Grass seed (x); Wildflower seed (x); Cacti or succulents

Vermont Wildflower Farm
Dept. BK, Rt. 7
Charlotte, VT 05445-0005
(802)425-3500
Percentage of the business in native species: 70%
Is a catalog or plant list available: Yes
What is the catalog fee, if any: N/A
Type of business: Retail (x); Wholesale (x); Mail Order (x)
Primary plant focus: Trees & shrubs; Herbaceous wildflowers; Grass
seed; Wildflower seed (x); Cacti or succulents

Abundant Life Seed Foundation
P. O. Box 772
1029 Lawrence
Port Townsend, WA 98368
(206)385-5660
Percentage of the business in native species: 100%
Is a catalog or plant list available: Yes
What is the catalog fee, if any: $1.00
Type of business: Retail (x); Wholesale (x); Mail Order (x)
Primary plant focus: Trees & shrubs (x); Herbaceous wildflowers (x);
Grass seed; Wildflower seed (x); Cacti or succulents

Aldrich Berry Farm & Nursery, Inc.
190 Aldrich Road
Mossyrock, WA 98564
(206)983-3138
Percentage of the business in native species: N/A
Is a catalog or plant list available: Yes
What is the catalog fee, if any: N/A
Type of business: Retail; Wholesale (x); Mail Order
Primary plant focus: Trees & shrubs; Herbaceous wildflowers; Grass seed
(x); Wildflower seed; Cacti or succulents

Bear Creek Nursery
P. O. Box 411
Bear Creek Road
Northport, WA 99157-0411
Percentage of the business in native species: 50%
Is a catalog or plant list available: Yes
What is the catalog fee, if any: Two first-class stamps
Type of business: Retail (x); Wholesale (x); Mail Order (x)
Primary plant focus: Trees & shrubs (x); Herbaceous wildflowers; Grass
seed; Wildflower seed; Cacti or succulents

Fancy Fronds (ferns only)
1911 4th Ave. W
Seattle, WA 98119
(206)284-5332
Percentage of the business in native species: 10%
Is a catalog or plant list available: Yes
What is the catalog fee, if any: $1.00
Type of business: Retail (x); Wholesale; Mail Order (x)
Primary plant focus: Trees & shrubs; Herbaceous wildflowers (x); Grass
seed; Wildflower seed; Cacti or succulents

Foliage Gardens
2003 128 Avenue SE
Bellevue, WA 98005
(206)747-2998
Percentage of the business in native species: 30%
Is a catalog or plant list available: Yes
What is the catalog fee, if any: $1.00
Type of business: Retail (x); Wholesale; Mail Order (x)
Primary plant focus: Trees & shrubs; Herbaceous wildflowers (x); Grass seed; Wildflower seed; Cacti or succulents

Frosty Hollow
P. O Box 53
Langley, WA 98260
(206)221-2332
Percentage of the business in native species: 90%
Is a catalog or plant list available: Yes
What is the catalog fee, if any: $1.00
Type of business: Retail (x); Wholesale (x); Mail Order (x)
Primary plant focus: Trees & shrubs (x); Herbaceous wildflowers (x); Grass seed; Wildflower seed (x); Cacti or succulents

Julius Rosso Wholesale Nursery Co.
6404 Ellis Ave. S
P. O. Box 80345
Seattle, WA 98108
(800)832-1888
Percentage of the business in native species: 10%
Is a catalog or plant list available: Yes
What is the catalog fee, if any: N/A
Type of business: Retail; Wholesale (x); Mail Order
Primary plant focus: Trees & shrubs (x); Herbaceous wildflowers; Grass seed (x); Wildflower seed; Cacti or succulents

Plants of the Wild
P. O. Box 866
Tekoa, WA 99033
(509)284-2848
Percentage of the business in native species: 95%
Is a catalog or plant list available: Yes
What is the catalog fee, if any: $1.00
Type of business: Retail; Wholesale (x); Mail Order
Primary plant focus: Trees & shrubs (x); Herbaceous wildflowers (x); Grass seed (x); Wildflower seed; Cacti or succulents

Silvaseed Company
P. O. Box 118
317 James St.
Roy, WA 98580
(206)843-2246
Percentage of the business in native species: 95%
Is a catalog or plant list available: Yes
What is the catalog fee, if any: SASE
Type of business: Retail; Wholesale (x); Mail Order
Primary plant focus: Trees & shrubs (x); Herbaceous wildflowers; Grass seed; Wildflower seed; Cacti or succulents

Boehlke's Woodland Gardens
W140 N10829 Country Aire Road
Germantown, WI 53022
Percentage of the business in native species: 90%
Is a catalog or plant list available: Yes
What is the catalog fee, if any: $1.00
Type of business: Retail (x); Wholesale (x); Mail Order (x)
Primary plant focus: Trees & shrubs; Herbaceous wildflowers (x); Grass seed; Wildflower seed; Cacti or succulents

Country Wetlands Nursery
P. O. Box 126
Muskego, WI 53150
(414)679-1268
Percentage of the business in native species: 95%
Is a catalog or plant list available: Yes
What is the catalog fee, if any: $2.00
Type of business: Retail (x); Wholesale (x); Mail Order (x)
Primary plant focus: Trees & shrubs (x); Herbaceous wildflowers (x); Grass seed (x); Wildflower seed (x); Cacti or succulents

CRM Ecosystems, Inc./Prairie Ridge Nursery
9738 Overland Road
Mount Horeb, WI 53572
(608)437-5245
Percentage of the business in native species: 100%
Is a catalog or plant list available: Yes
What is the catalog fee, if any: $2.00
Type of business: Retail (x); Wholesale (x); Mail Order (x)
Primary plant focus: Trees & shrubs; Herbaceous wildflowers (x); Grass seed (x); Wildflower seed (x); Cacti or succulents

Kettle Moraine Natural Landscaping
W996 Birchwood Dr.
Campbellsport, WI 53010
(414)533-8939
Percentage of the business in native species: 100%
Is a catalog or plant list available: Yes
What is the catalog fee, if any: Free
Type of business: Retail (x); Wholesale; Mail Order (x)
Primary plant focus: Trees & shrubs; Herbaceous wildflowers; Grass seed (x); Wildflower seed (x); Cacti or succulents

L. L. Olds Seed Company
P. O. Box 7790
2901 Packers Ave.
Madison, WI 53707-7790
(608)249-9291
Percentage of the business in native species: Small
Is a catalog or plant list available: Yes
What is the catalog fee, if any: Free
Type of business: Retail; Wholesale (x); Mail Order
Primary plant focus: Trees & shrubs; Herbaceous wildflowers; Grass seed (x); Wildflower seed (x); Cacti or succulents

Little Valley Farm
Rt. 3, Box 544
Spring Green, WI 53588
(608)935-3324
Percentage of the business in native species: 100%
Is a catalog or plant list available: Yes
What is the catalog fee, if any: $0.25
Type of business: Retail; Wholesale; Mail Order (x)
Primary plant focus: Trees & shrubs (x); Herbaceous wildflowers (x); Grass seed (x); Wildflower seed (x); Cacti or succulents

Milaeger's Gardens
4838 Douglas Ave.
Racine, WI 53402-2498
(414)639-2371
Percentage of the business in native species: 10%
Is a catalog or plant list available: Yes
What is the catalog fee, if any: N/A
Type of business: Retail (x); Wholesale (x); Mail Order (x)
Primary plant focus: Trees & shrubs; Herbaceous wildflowers (x); Grass seed; Wildflower seed; Cacti or succulents

Nature's Nursery
6125 Mathewson Road
Mazomanie, WI 53560
(608)795-4920
Percentage of the business in native species: 100%
Is a catalog or plant list available: Yes
What is the catalog fee, if any: Free
Type of business: Retail (x); Wholesale; Mail Order (x)
Primary plant focus: Trees & shrubs; Herbaceous wildflowers (x); Grass
seed (x); Wildflower seed (x); Cacti or succulents

Prairie Future Seed Company
P. O. Box 644
Menomonee Falls, WI 53052
(414)246-4019
Percentage of the business in native species: 93%
Is a catalog or plant list available: Yes
What is the catalog fee, if any: $3.00
Type of business: Retail (x); Wholesale (x); Mail Order (x)
Primary plant focus: Trees & shrubs; Herbaceous wildflowers; Grass seed
(x); Wildflower seed (x); Cacti or succulents

Prairie Nursery
P. O. Box 306
Westfield, WI 53964
(608)296-3679
Percentage of the business in native species: 100%
Is a catalog or plant list available: Yes
What is the catalog fee, if any: $3.00
Type of business: Retail (x); Wholesale (x); Mail Order (x)
Primary plant focus: Trees & shrubs; Herbaceous wildflowers (x); Grass
seed (x); Wildflower seed (x); Cacti or succulents

Prairie Seed Source
P. O. Box 83
North Lake, WI 53064-0083
(414)673-7166
Percentage of the business in native species: 100%
Is a catalog or plant list available: Yes
What is the catalog fee, if any: $1.00
Type of business: Retail (x); Wholesale; Mail Order (x)
Primary plant focus: Trees & shrubs; Herbaceous wildflowers; Grass seed (x); Wildflower seed (x); Cacti or succulents

Reeseville Ridge Nursery
P. O. Box 171
309 S. Main St.
Reeseville, WI 53579
(414)927-3291
Percentage of the business in native species: 50%
Is a catalog or plant list available: Yes
What is the catalog fee, if any: Free
Type of business: Retail (x); Wholesale (x); Mail Order
Primary plant focus: Trees & shrubs (x); Herbaceous wildflowers; Grass seed; Wildflower seed; Cacti or succulents

Retzer Nature Center
W284 S1530 Road DT
Waukesha, WI 53188
(414)521-5407
Percentage of the business in native species: 98%
Is a catalog or plant list available: Yes
What is the catalog fee, if any: Free
Type of business: Retail (x); Wholesale (x); Mail Order
Primary plant focus: Trees & shrubs (x); Herbaceous wildflowers (x); Grass seed (x); Wildflower seed (x); Cacti or succulents

Shady Acres Nursery, Inc.
5725 S. Martin Road
New Berlin, WI 53146
(414)679-1610
Percentage of the business in native species: Small
Is a catalog or plant list available: Yes
What is the catalog fee, if any: $1.00
Type of business: Retail (x); Wholesale (x); Mail Order
Primary plant focus: Trees & shrubs; Herbaceous wildflowers (x); Grass seed (x); Wildflower seed; Cacti or succulents

Wehr Nature Center
9701 W. College Ave.
Franklin, WI 53132
(414)425-8550
Percentage of the business in native species: 100%
Is a catalog or plant list available: Yes
What is the catalog fee, if any: Free
Type of business: Retail (x); Wholesale; Mail Order
Primary plant focus: Trees & shrubs; Herbaceous wildflowers; Grass seed; Wildflower seed (x); Cacti or succulents

Mountain West Seeds
P. O. Box 1471
Cheyenne, WY 82003-1471
(307)634-6328
Percentage of the business in native species: 100%
Is a catalog or plant list available: Yes
What is the catalog fee, if any: First class postage
Type of business: Retail (x); Wholesale; Mail Order (x)
Primary plant focus: Trees & shrubs; Herbaceous wildflowers; Grass seed; Wildflower seed (x); Cacti or succulents

Wind River Seed, Inc.
Rt. 1 Box 97
3075 Lane 51-1/2
Manderson, WY 82432-9605
(307)568-3325
Percentage of the business in native species: 90%
Is a catalog or plant list available: Yes
What is the catalog fee, if any: None
Type of business: Retail (x); Wholesale (x); Mail Order (x)
Primary plant focus: Trees & shrubs (x); Herbaceous wildflowers (x); Grass seed (x); Wildflower seed (x); Cacti or succulents

Dodecatheon pulchellum

Landscape Architects & Designers Who Use Native Plants

Land Design North
1021 W. 25th Ave.
Anchorage, AK 99503
(907)276-5885
Area served: City, State (x), Regional, National
Work with natives: 75-100% (x); 50-75%; 25-50%; 10-25%; 10% or less
Services: Design (x); Landuse planning (x); Specifications (x); Installation; Site analysis (x); Maintenance (x)
Specialization: Residential (x); Commercial (x); Parkland (x); Corporate grounds (x); Nature centers (x); Industrial projects (x); Roadside (x)

Bowden Design Group, Inc.
7100 E. Lincoln Dr., Suite A-106
Scottsdale, AZ 85251
(602)443-0223
Area served: City, State (x), Regional, National
Work with natives: 75-100% (x); 50-75%; 25-50%; 10-25%; 10% or less
Services: Design (x); Landuse planning (x); Specifications (x); Installation; Site analysis (x); Maintenance (x)
Specialization: Residential (x); Commercial (x); Parkland; Corporate grounds; Nature centers; Industrial projects; Roadside (x)

C. F. Shuler, Inc.
15020 N. Hayden Rd., #204
Scottsdale, AZ 85260
(602)483-0535
Area served: City (x), State (x), Regional (x), National
Work with natives: 75-100% (x); 50-75%; 25-50%; 10-25%; 10% or less
Services: Design; Landuse planning; Specifications; Installation; Site analysis; Maintenance
Specialization: Residential (x); Commercial (x); Parkland (x); Corporate grounds (x); Nature centers; Industrial projects; Roadside (x)

Rogers, Gladwin & Rothman
The Acacia Group, Inc.
382 S. Convent Ave.
Tucson, AZ 85701
(602)622-2302
Area served: City, State, Regional (x), National
Work with natives: 75-100%; 50-75% (x); 25-50%; 10-25%; 10% or less
Services: Design (x); Landuse planning (x); Specifications (x); Installation; Site analysis (x); Maintenance (x)
Specialization: Residential (x); Commercial (x); Parkland (x); Corporate grounds (x); Nature centers; Industrial projects (x); Roadside (x)

Taylor Made Landscape Development
939 Hemlock Ave.
Prescott, AZ 86303
(602)445-4624
Area served: City, State (x), Regional, National
Work with natives: 75-100%; 50-75%; 25-50% (x); 10-25%; 10% or less
Services: Design (x); Landuse planning (x); Specifications (x); Installation (x);
Site analysis (x); Maintenance (x)
Specialization: Residential (x); Commercial; Parkland; Corporate grounds;
Nature centers (x); Industrial projects; Roadside

Western Sere
P. O. Box 1062
Casa Grande, AZ 85222
(602)836-8246
Area served: City, State, Regional (x), National
Work with natives: 75-100% (x); 50-75%; 25-50%; 10-25%; 10% or less
Services: Design; Landuse planning; Specifications; Installation; Site analysis;
Maintenance
Specialization: Residential (x); Commercial (x); Parkland (x); Corporate
grounds (x); Nature centers (x); Industrial projects (x); Roadside (x)

Good Earth Landscape Design
32977 Wintermute Lane
Tollhouse, CA 93667
(209)855-3513
Area served: City, State, Regional (x), National
Work with natives: 75-100%; 50-75% (x); 25-50%; 10-25%; 10% or less
Services: Design (x); Landuse planning; Specifications; Installation (x); Site
analysis; Maintenance
Specialization: Residential (x); Commercial; Parkland (x); Corporate grounds;
Nature centers; Industrial projects; Roadside (x)

Graeber Gardens
115 Monterey Salinas Highway
Salinas, CA 93908
(408)455-1876
Area served: City (x), State, Regional, National
Work with natives: 75-100%; 50-75%; 25-50% (x); 10-25%; 10% or less
Services: Design (x); Landuse planning; Specifications; Installation (x); Site analysis; Maintenance (x)
Specialization: Residential (x); Commercial (x); Parkland; Corporate grounds; Nature centers; Industrial projects; Roadside

Habitat Restoration
3234 'H' Ashford St.
San Diego, CA 92111
(619)279-8769
Area served: City, State (x), Regional, National
Work with natives: 75-100% (x); 50-75%; 25-50%; 10-25%; 10% or less
Services: Design (x); Landuse planning (x); Specifications (x); Installation (x); Site analysis (x); Maintenance (x)
Specialization: Residential; Commercial; Parkland (x); Corporate grounds; Nature centers (x); Industrial projects; Roadside

Habitat Restoration Group, The
6001 Butler Lane, Suite 1
Scotts Valley, CA 95066-3542
Area served: City, State (x), Regional, National
Work with natives: 75-100% (x); 50-75%; 25-50%; 10-25%; 10% or less
Services: Design (x); Landuse planning (x); Specifications (x); Installation (x); Site analysis (x); Maintenance (x)
Specialization: Residential; Commercial; Parkland (x); Corporate grounds; Nature centers (x); Industrial projects (x); Roadside (x)

Lost West
4602 Los Feliz Blvd., #102
Los Angeles, CA 90027
(213)913-3737
Area served: City (x), State, Regional, National
Work with natives: 75-100% (x); 50-75%; 25-50%; 10-25%; 10% or less
Services: Design (x); Landuse planning (x); Specifications (x); Installation (x); Site analysis (x); Maintenance (x)
Specialization: Residential (x); Commercial; Parkland (x); Corporate grounds; Nature centers (x); Industrial projects; Roadside

Pacific Coast Seed, Inc.
7074-D Commerce Circle
Pleasanton, CA 94588
(415)463-1188
Area served: City, State, Regional (x), National
Work with natives: 75-100%; 50-75%; 25-50%; 10-25% (x); 10% or less
Services: Design; Landuse planning; Specifications; Installation; Site analysis; Maintenance
Specialization: Residential; Commercial (x); Parkland; Corporate grounds (x); Nature centers; Industrial projects (x); Roadside (x)

Pacific Open-Space, Inc.
P. O. Box 744
Petaluma, CA 94953-0744
(707)769-1213
Area served: City, State (x), Regional (x), National
Work with natives: 75-100% (x); 50-75%; 25-50%; 10-25%; 10% or less
Services: Design (x); Landuse planning (x); Specifications (x); Installation (x); Site analysis; Maintenance (x)
Specialization: Residential; Commercial; Parkland (x); Corporate grounds (x); Nature centers (x); Industrial projects (x); Roadside (x)

Thasos Environmental Group
P. O. Box 3546
Chico, CA 95927-3546
(916)345-1342
Area served: City (x), State (x), Regional, National
Work with natives: 75-100% (x); 50-75%; 25-50%; 10-25%; 10% or less
Services: Design (x); Landuse planning (x); Specifications (x); Installation; Site analysis (x); Maintenance
Specialization: Residential; Commercial; Parkland (x); Corporate grounds (x); Nature centers (x); Industrial projects (x); Roadside (x)

The Landscape Ecology Group
16751 Greenview Lane
Huntington Beach, CA 92649
(714)846-6910
Area served: City, State (x), Regional, National
Work with natives: 75-100% (x); 50-75%; 25-50%; 10-25%; 10% or less
Services: Design (x); Landuse planning; Specifications (x); Installation (x); Site analysis (x); Maintenance (x)
Specialization: Residential; Commercial; Parkland; Corporate grounds; Nature centers; Industrial projects (x); Roadside (x)

Eletes
636 Gaylord
Denver, CO 80206
(303)333-3024
Area served: City (x), State, Regional, National
Work with natives: 75-100%; 50-75% (x); 25-50%; 10-25%; 10% or less
Services: Design (x); Landuse planning (x); Specifications (x); Installation; Site analysis; Maintenance (x)
Specialization: Residential (x); Commercial (x); Parkland; Corporate grounds; Nature centers (x); Industrial projects; Roadside (x)

Matrix Gardens
1545 Redwood Ave.
Boulder, CO 80304
(303)443-0284
Area served: City (x), State, Regional (x), National
Work with natives: 75-100%; 50-75% (x); 25-50%; 10-25%; 10% or less
Services: Design (x); Landuse planning (x); Specifications; Installation (x); Site analysis (x); Maintenance
Specialization: Residential (x); Commercial; Parkland; Corporate grounds; Nature centers; Industrial projects; Roadside

MK Environmental Services
1700 Lincoln St., #4800
Denver, CO 80203
(303)860-8621
Area served: City, State, Regional (x), National
Work with natives: 75-100% (x); 50-75%; 25-50%; 10-25%; 10% or less
Services: Design (x); Landuse planning (x); Specifications (x); Installation (x); Site analysis (x); Maintenance (x)
Specialization: Residential; Commercial; Parkland (x); Corporate grounds; Nature centers (x); Industrial projects (x); Roadside (x)

N.E.S., Inc.
1040 S. 8th St.
Colorado Springs, CO 80906
(719)471-0073
Area served: City, State, Regional (x), National
Work with natives: 75-100%; 50-75% (x); 25-50%; 10-25%; 10% or less
Services: Design (x); Landuse planning (x); Specifications (x); Installation; Site analysis (x); Maintenance (x)
Specialization: Residential (x); Commercial (x); Parkland (x); Corporate grounds (x); Nature centers (x); Industrial projects (x); Roadside (x)

Rocky Mountain Trees & Landscaping
P. O. Box 1336
305 Buckley Dr.
Crested Butte, CO 81224
(303)349-6361
Area served: City, State (x), Regional, National
Work with natives: 75-100%; 50-75% (x); 25-50%; 10-25%; 10% or less
Services: Design (x); Landuse planning (x); Specifications (x); Installation (x); Site analysis; Maintenance (x)
Specialization: Residential (x); Commercial (x); Parkland (x); Corporate grounds; Nature centers; Industrial projects; Roadside (x)

A.E. Bye Associates-Landscape Architects
533 E. Post Rd.
Cos Cob, CT 06807
(203)661-8277
Area served: City, State, Regional (x), National
Work with natives: 75-100% (x); 50-75%; 25-50%; 10-25%; 10% or less
Services: Design (x); Landuse planning; Specifications; Installation (x); Site analysis (x); Maintenance
Specialization: Residential (x); Commercial (x); Parkland (x); Corporate grounds (x); Nature centers; Industrial projects; Roadside

Ecological Consultants, Inc.
5121 Ehrlich Rd., Suite 103A
Tampa, FL 33624
(813)264-5859
Area served: City, State (x), Regional, National
Work with natives: 75-100% (x); 50-75%; 25-50%; 10-25%; 10% or less
Services: Design (x); Landuse planning; Specifications (x); Installation (x); Site analysis (x); Maintenance (x)
Specialization: Residential (x); Commercial (x); Parkland (x); Corporate grounds (x); Nature centers (x); Industrial projects (x); Roadside

Native Nurseries of Tallahassee, Inc.
1661 Centerville Rd.
Tallahassee, FL 32308
(904)386-2747
Area served: City (x), State, Regional, National
Work with natives: 75-100% (x); 50-75%; 25-50%; 10-25%; 10% or less
Services: Design (x); Landuse planning; Specifications; Installation (x); Site analysis; Maintenance
Specialization: Residential (x); Commercial; Parkland; Corporate grounds; Nature centers (x); Industrial projects; Roadside

Wetlands Management, Inc.
P. O. Box 1122
Jensen Beach, FL 34958-1122
(407)334-1643
Area served: City, State, Regional (x), National
Work with natives: 75-100% (x); 50-75%; 25-50%; 10-25%; 10% or less
Services: Design; Landuse planning; Specifications; Installation; Site analysis; Maintenance
Specialization: Residential; Commercial; Parkland; Corporate grounds; Nature centers; Industrial projects; Roadside

Leah Pine Designs
340 Talmadge Dr.
Athens, GA 30606
(404)354-3982
Area served: City, State, Regional (x), National
Work with natives: 75-100% (x); 50-75%; 25-50%; 10-25%; 10% or less
Services: Design; Landuse planning; Specifications; Installation; Site analysis; Maintenance
Specialization: Residential (x); Commercial (x); Parkland; Corporate grounds (x); Nature centers (x); Industrial projects; Roadside

Compass Plant Consultants
P. O. Box 298
Prairie City, IA 50228
Area served: City (x), State (x), Regional, National
Work with natives: 75-100% (x); 50-75%; 25-50%; 10-25%; 10% or less
Services: Design (x); Landuse planning (x); Specifications (x); Installation (x); Site analysis (x); Maintenance (x)
Specialization: Residential (x); Commercial (x); Parkland (x); Corporate grounds (x); Nature centers (x); Industrial projects (x); Roadside (x)

Don Brigham Plus Associates
128 Main, #1
Lewiston, ID 83501
(208)743-7553
Area served: City, State, Regional (x), National
Work with natives: 75-100%; 50-75%; 25-50% (x); 10-25%; 10% or less
Services: Design (x); Landuse planning (x); Specifications (x); Installation; Site analysis (x); Maintenance
Specialization: Residential (x); Commercial (x); Parkland (x); Corporate grounds; Nature centers; Industrial projects; Roadside

Karin Wisiol & Associates
614 Indian Rd.
Glenview, IL 60025
(708)729-7786
Area served: City, State, Regional (x), National (x)
Work with natives: 75-100%; 50-75%; 25-50%; 10-25%; 10% or less
Services: Design; Landuse planning; Specifications; Installation; Site analysis; Maintenance
Specialization: Residential; Commercial; Parkland (x); Corporate grounds; Nature centers (x); Industrial projects (x); Roadside (x)

Kestrel Design Group, Inc., The
P. O. Box 910
Wheeling, IL 60090-0910
(708)520-0063
Area served: City, State, Regional (x), National
Work with natives: 75-100% (x); 50-75%; 25-50%; 10-25%; 10% or less
Services: Design (x); Landuse planning (x); Specifications (x); Installation; Site analysis (x); Maintenance (x)
Specialization: Residential (x); Commercial (x); Parkland (x); Corporate grounds (x); Nature centers (x); Industrial projects (x); Roadside (x)

Native Landscapes
1947 Madron Rd.
Rockford, IL 61107-1716
(815)637-6622
Area served: City, State (x), Regional, National
Work with natives: 75-100% (x); 50-75%; 25-50%; 10-25%; 10% or less
Services: Design; Landuse planning (x); Specifications; Installation; Site analysis (x); Maintenance
Specialization: Residential; Commercial; Parkland (x); Corporate grounds; Nature centers; Industrial projects; Roadside

Natural Garden, The
38 W. 443 Highway 64
St. Charles, IL 60175
(708)584-0150
Area served: City, State, Regional (x), National
Work with natives: 75-100%; 50-75% (x); 25-50%; 10-25%; 10% or less
Services: Design (x); Landuse planning (x); Specifications (x); Installation (x); Site analysis (x); Maintenance (x)
Specialization: Residential (x); Commercial (x); Parkland (x); Corporate grounds (x); Nature centers (x); Industrial projects; Roadside (x)

Dahl & Associates, Inc.
4420 Soldiers Home Rd.
West Lafayette, IN 47906
(317)494-1330
Area served: City, State, Regional (x), National
Work with natives: 75-100%; 50-75%; 25-50% (x); 10-25%; 10% or less
Services: Design (x); Landuse planning (x); Specifications; Installation; Site analysis (x); Maintenance
Specialization: Residential (x); Commercial; Parkland (x); Corporate grounds; Nature centers; Industrial projects (x); Roadside

Song Dog Consulting
Rt. 2 Box 185
Velpen, IN 47590
(812)536-3574
Area served: City, State, Regional, National
Work with natives: 75-100% (x); 50-75%; 25-50%; 10-25%; 10% or less
Services: Design (x); Landuse planning; Specifications; Installation (x); Site analysis (x); Maintenance (x)
Specialization: Residential (x); Commercial (x); Parkland (x); Corporate grounds (x); Nature centers (x); Industrial projects; Roadside (x)

Gardenworks
1407 Blue Vale Way
Louisville, KY 40222-0385
(502)426-0742
Area served: City, State, Regional (x), National
Work with natives: 75-100%; 50-75% (x); 25-50%; 10-25%; 10% or less
Services: Design (x); Landuse planning; Specifications; Installation (x); Site analysis; Maintenance (x)
Specialization: Residential (x); Commercial; Parkland; Corporate grounds; Nature centers; Industrial projects; Roadside

Natives Landscape Corporation
320 N. Theard St.
Covington, LA 70433
(504)892-5424
Area served: City, State, Regional (x), National
Work with natives: 75-100% (x); 50-75%; 25-50%; 10-25%; 10% or less
Services: Design (x); Landuse planning (x); Specifications (x); Installation (x); Site analysis (x); Maintenance (x)
Specialization: Residential (x); Commercial (x); Parkland; Corporate grounds (x); Nature centers (x); Industrial projects; Roadside (x)

Patrick Moore, ASLA Landscape Architect
301 Jackson St., Suite 304
Alexandria, LA 71301
(318)445-2825
Area served: City, State, Regional (x), National
Work with natives: 75-100%; 50-75% (x); 25-50%; 10-25%; 10% or less
Services: Design; Landuse planning; Specifications; Installation; Site analysis; Maintenance (x)
Specialization: Residential (x); Commercial (x); Parkland (x); Corporate grounds (x); Nature centers; Industrial projects (x); Roadside

Prairie Basse
Rt. 2 Box 491-F
Carencro, LA 70520
(318)896-9187
Area served: City, State (x), Regional, National
Work with natives: 75-100%; 50-75%; 25-50%; 10-25%; 10% or less
Services: Design; Landuse planning; Specifications; Installation; Site analysis; Maintenance
Specialization: Residential; Commercial; Parkland; Corporate grounds; Nature centers; Industrial projects; Roadside

Wettanda Ecological Services
P. O. Box 701
Madisonville, LA 70447
(504)845-0661
Area served: City, State (x), Regional, National
Work with natives: 75-100% (x); 50-75%; 25-50%; 10-25%; 10% or less
Services: Design; Landuse planning; Specifications; Installation; Site analysis; Maintenance
Specialization: Residential (x); Commercial (x); Parkland; Corporate grounds; Nature centers (x); Industrial projects (x); Roadside

Blisscapes
139 Stephen St.
South Dartmouth, MA 02748
(508)993-0049
Area served: City (x), State (x), Regional (x), National (x)
Work with natives: 75-100%; 50-75% (x); 25-50%; 10-25%; 10% or less
Services: Design (x); Landuse planning (x); Specifications; Installation (x); Site analysis (x); Maintenance (x)
Specialization: Residential (x); Commercial (x); Parkland (x); Corporate grounds (x); Nature centers (x); Industrial projects (x); Roadside

Wesley Williams Horticulture, Landscaping, Tree Service
P. O. Box 208
Ashby, MA 01431
(603)878-1926
Area served: City (x), State (x), Regional (x), National
Work with natives: 75-100% (x); 50-75%; 25-50%; 10-25%; 10% or less
Services: Design (x); Landuse planning (x); Specifications (x); Installation (x); Site analysis (x); Maintenance (x)
Specialization: Residential (x); Commercial (x); Parkland (x); Corporate grounds (x); Nature centers (x); Industrial projects (x); Roadside (x)

Envirens, Inc.
1927 York Rd.
Timonium, MD 21093
(301)560-2288
Area served: City, State, Regional (x), National
Work with natives: 75-100% (x); 50-75%; 25-50%; 10-25%; 10% or less
Services: Design (x); Landuse planning (x); Specifications; Installation (x); Site analysis (x); Maintenance (x)
Specialization: Residential (x); Commercial (x); Parkland (x); Corporate grounds (x); Nature centers (x); Industrial projects (x); Roadside (x)

Environmental Concern, Inc.
P. O. Box P
210 W. Chew Ave.
St. Michaels, MD 21663
(301)745-9620
Area served: City, State, Regional (x), National
Work with natives: 75-100% (x); 50-75%; 25-50%; 10-25%; 10% or less
Services: Design; Landuse planning; Specifications; Installation; Site analysis; Maintenance
Specialization: Residential; Commercial; Parkland; Corporate grounds; Nature centers; Industrial projects; Roadside

Joan Lutz Kuckkahn, Landscape Architect
23 Welwyn Way
Rockville, MD 20850
(301)340-0031
Area served: City, State, Regional (x), National
Work with natives: 75-100%; 50-75%; 25-50%; 10-25%; 10% or less (x)
Services: Design (x); Landuse planning (x); Specifications (x); Installation; Site analysis (x); Maintenance (x)
Specialization: Residential (x); Commercial (x); Parkland (x); Corporate grounds (x); Nature centers (x); Industrial projects (x); Roadside (x)

John E. Harms, Jr. & Associates, Inc.
P. O. Box 5
90 Ritchie Highway
Pasadena, MD 21122
(301)647-6000
Area served: City, State (x), Regional, National
Work with natives: 75-100%; 50-75%; 25-50%; 10-25% (x); 10% or less
Services: Design (x); Landuse planning (x); Specifications (x); Installation; Site analysis (x); Maintenance
Specialization: Residential (x); Commercial (x); Parkland (x); Corporate grounds; Nature centers; Industrial projects; Roadside

Redman/Johnston Associates, Ltd.
29515 Canvasback Dr., Unit 2
Easton, MD 21601
(301)822-9630
Area served: City, State, Regional (x), National
Work with natives: 75-100%; 50-75%; 25-50% (x); 10-25%; 10% or less
Services: Design (x); Landuse planning (x); Specifications (x); Installation; Site analysis (x); Maintenance (x)
Specialization: Residential (x); Commercial (x); Parkland (x); Corporate grounds; Nature centers (x); Industrial projects; Roadside

Landscape Design Associates
10 Main St., Box 1007
Northeast Harbor, ME 04662-1007
(207)276-5674
Area served: City, State, Regional (x), National
Work with natives: 75-100%; 50-75% (x); 25-50%; 10-25%; 10% or less
Services: Design (x); Landuse planning (x); Specifications (x); Installation; Site analysis (x); Maintenance (x)
Specialization: Residential (x); Commercial; Parkland (x); Corporate grounds; Nature centers (x); Industrial projects (x); Roadside (x)

Normandeau Associates Inc.
P. O. Box 202
38 Lafayette St.
Yarmouth, ME 04096
(207)846-3598
Area served: City, State (x), Regional, National
Work with natives: 75-100% (x); 50-75%; 25-50%; 10-25%; 10% or less
Services: Design; Landuse planning; Specifications; Installation; Site analysis; Maintenance
Specialization: Residential; Commercial; Parkland; Corporate grounds; Nature centers; Industrial projects; Roadside

Plants of Maine, Inc.
P. O. Box 126
South Hiram Road
Cornish, ME 04020
(207)625-8303
Area served: City, State, Regional (x), National
Work with natives: 75-100%; 50-75%; 25-50% (x); 10-25%; 10% or less
Services: Design (x); Landuse planning; Specifications; Installation; Site analysis; Maintenance (x)
Specialization: Residential (x); Commercial; Parkland; Corporate grounds; Nature centers (x); Industrial projects; Roadside

Grass Roots, Inc.
P. O. Box 4001
16262 Chandler Rd.
East Lansing, MI 48826
(517)337-2405
Area served: City (x), State, Regional, National
Work with natives: 75-100%; 50-75% (x); 25-50%; 10-25%; 10% or less
Services: Design (x); Landuse planning; Specifications (x); Installation (x); Site analysis (x); Maintenance (x)
Specialization: Residential (x); Commercial (x); Parkland; Corporate grounds; Nature centers; Industrial projects; Roadside

Johnson Johnson and Roy, Inc.
110 Miller
Ann Arbor, MI 48104
(313)662-4457
Area served: City, State, Regional, National (x)
Work with natives: 75-100%; 50-75%; 25-50% (x); 10-25%; 10% or less
Services: Design (x); Landuse planning (x); Specifications (x); Installation; Site analysis (x); Maintenance
Specialization: Residential (x); Commercial (x); Parkland (x); Corporate grounds (x); Nature centers (x); Industrial projects (x); Roadside

Evergreen EnergyScapes
3849 Pillsbury Ave. S
Minneapolis, MN 55409-1222
(612)823-4012
Area served: City, State, Regional (x), National
Work with natives: 75-100% (x); 50-75%; 25-50%; 10-25%; 10% or less
Services: Design (x); Landuse planning (x); Specifications; Installation (x); Site analysis (x); Maintenance (x)
Specialization: Residential (x); Commercial (x); Parkland; Corporate grounds; Nature centers; Industrial projects; Roadside

James Robin, Landscape Architect
23420 Park St.
Excelsior, MN 55331
(612)474-3946
Area served: City (x), State, Regional, National
Work with natives: 75-100%; 50-75%; 25-50%; 10-25%; 10% or less (x)
Services: Design (x); Landuse planning (x); Specifications (x); Installation (x); Site analysis (x); Maintenance
Specialization: Residential (x); Commercial (x); Parkland (x); Corporate grounds (x); Nature centers (x); Industrial projects; Roadside

Kevin G. Norby & Associates, Inc.
6001 Redwing Lane
Chanhassen, MN 55317
(612)474-0403
Area served: City, State (x), Regional, National
Work with natives: 75-100% (x); 50-75%; 25-50%; 10-25%; 10% or less
Services: Design (x); Landuse planning (x); Specifications (x); Installation; Site analysis (x); Maintenance
Specialization: Residential (x); Commercial (x); Parkland (x); Corporate grounds (x); Nature centers (x); Industrial projects; Roadside

Landscape Alternatives, Inc.
1465 N. Pascal St.
St. Paul, MN 55108
(612)488-3142
Area served: City, State, Regional (x), National
Work with natives: 75-100% (x); 50-75%; 25-50%; 10-25%; 10% or less
Services: Design (x); Landuse planning (x); Specifications (x); Installation (x); Site analysis (x); Maintenance (x)
Specialization: Residential (x); Commercial (x); Parkland (x); Corporate grounds (x); Nature centers (x); Industrial projects; Roadside (x)

Native Landscapes
407 Second St. NE
Minneapolis, MN 55413
(612)379-3106
Area served: City, State (x), Regional, National
Work with natives: 75-100% (x); 50-75%; 25-50%; 10-25%; 10% or less
Services: Design (x); Landuse planning; Specifications; Installation (x); Site analysis (x); Maintenance
Specialization: Residential (x); Commercial; Parkland; Corporate grounds; Nature centers (x); Industrial projects; Roadside (x)

Prairie Hill Wildflowers
Rt. 1 Box 191-A
Ellendale, MN 56026
(507)451-7791
Area served: City, State, Regional (x), National
Work with natives: 75-100% (x); 50-75%; 25-50%; 10-25%; 10% or less
Services: Design (x); Landuse planning (x); Specifications (x); Installation (x); Site analysis (x); Maintenance (x)
Specialization: Residential (x); Commercial (x); Parkland (x); Corporate grounds (x); Nature centers; Industrial projects; Roadside

Prairie Restorations, Inc.
P. O. Box 327
Princeton, MN 55371
(612)389-4342
Area served: City, State (x), Regional, National
Work with natives: 75-100% (x); 50-75%; 25-50%; 10-25%; 10% or less
Services: Design (x); Landuse planning (x); Specifications (x); Installation (x); Site analysis (x); Maintenance (x)
Specialization: Residential (x); Commercial (x); Parkland (x); Corporate grounds (x); Nature centers (x); Industrial projects (x); Roadside (x)

Savanna Designs, Inc.
3511 Lake Elmo Ave.
Lake Elmo, MN 55042
(612)770-6910
Area served: City (x), State, Regional, National
Work with natives: 75-100%; 50-75% (x); 25-50%; 10-25%; 10% or less
Services: Design (x); Landuse planning; Specifications; Installation (x); Site analysis (x); Maintenance (x)
Specialization: Residential (x); Commercial (x); Parkland; Corporate grounds; Nature centers; Industrial projects; Roadside

Flick Brothers Seed Company
Rt. 1 Box 260
Kingsville, MO 64061
(816)597-3663 or (816)597-3458
Area served: City, State, Regional (x), National
Work with natives: 75-100%; 50-75% (x); 25-50%; 10-25%; 10% or less
Services: Design; Landuse planning (x); Specifications (x); Installation (x); Site analysis; Maintenance
Specialization: Residential (x); Commercial (x); Parkland (x); Corporate grounds (x); Nature centers (x); Industrial projects (x); Roadside (x)

The Crosby Arboretum
P. O. Box 190
Picayune, MS 39466
(601)799-0500
Area served: City, State, Regional (x), National
Work with natives: 75-100% (x); 50-75%; 25-50%; 10-25%; 10% or less
Services: Design (x); Landuse planning (x); Specifications; Installation; Site analysis (x); Maintenance (x)
Specialization: Residential (x); Commercial; Parkland (x); Corporate grounds (x); Nature centers (x); Industrial projects (x); Roadside (x)

BNG Consultants
Bitterroot Native Growers, Inc.
P. O. Box 566
Hamilton, MT 59840
(406)961-4991
Area served: City, State, Regional (x), National
Work with natives: 75-100% (x); 50-75%; 25-50%; 10-25%; 10% or less
Services: Design (x); Landuse planning; Specifications; Installation (x); Site analysis (x); Maintenance
Specialization: Residential; Commercial; Parkland; Corporate grounds; Nature centers; Industrial projects (x); Roadside (x)

Dennis Colliton, Landscape Architects
P. O. Box 5231
S.U. Station
Fargo, ND 58105-5231
(701)237-8508
Area served: City, State (x), Regional, National
Work with natives: 75-100%; 50-75% (x); 25-50%; 10-25%; 10% or less
Services: Design (x); Landuse planning (x); Specifications (x); Installation; Site analysis (x); Maintenance (x)
Specialization: Residential (x); Commercial (x); Parkland (x); Corporate grounds; Nature centers (x); Industrial projects; Roadside (x)

Living Earth Designs
4630 Saratoga St.
Omaha, NE 68104
(402)457-4540
Area served: City (x), State, Regional, National
Work with natives: 75-100% (x); 50-75%; 25-50%; 10-25%; 10% or less
Services: Design (x); Landuse planning; Specifications; Installation (x); Site analysis (x); Maintenance (x)
Specialization: Residential (x); Commercial; Parkland; Corporate grounds; Nature centers; Industrial projects; Roadside

Helen Hendrickson Heinrich, ASLA
71 Green Village Rd.
Madison, NJ 07940
(201)377-3956
Area served: City, State (x), Regional, National
Work with natives: 75-100% (x); 50-75%; 25-50%; 10-25%; 10% or less
Services: Design (x); Landuse planning (x); Specifications (x); Installation (x); Site analysis (x); Maintenance (x)
Specialization: Residential (x); Commercial (x); Parkland (x); Corporate grounds (x); Nature centers (x); Industrial projects (x); Roadside (x)

Natural Design Concepts
41 Ethel Place
Metuchen, NJ 08840
(908)549-7414
Area served: City (x), State (x), Regional (x), National
Work with natives: 75-100% (x); 50-75%; 25-50%; 10-25%; 10% or less
Services: Design (x); Landuse planning (x); Specifications; Installation; Site analysis (x); Maintenance
Specialization: Residential (x); Commercial (x); Parkland (x); Corporate grounds (x); Nature centers (x); Industrial projects; Roadside

Peter Ritchie & Associates
RD #4 Rt. 27
Princeton, NJ 08540
(609)924-4003
Area served: City, State (x), Regional, National
Work with natives: 75-100%; 50-75%; 25-50% (x); 10-25%; 10% or less
Services: Design (x); Landuse planning (x); Specifications (x); Installation; Site analysis (x); Maintenance
Specialization: Residential (x); Commercial (x); Parkland (x); Corporate grounds (x); Nature centers; Industrial projects; Roadside

Panfield Nurseries, Inc.
322 Southdown Rd.
Huntington, NY 11743
(516)427-0112
Area served: City, State, Regional (x), National
Work with natives: 75-100%; 50-75%; 25-50% (x); 10-25%; 10% or less
Services: Design (x); Landuse planning (x); Specifications; Installation (x); Site analysis (x); Maintenance (x)
Specialization: Residential (x); Commercial; Parkland; Corporate grounds; Nature centers; Industrial projects; Roadside

Elliott Enterprises
2580 Wellington Rd.
Cleveland, OH 44118
(216)371-1730
Area served: City (x), State, Regional, National
Work with natives: 75-100%; 50-75%; 25-50% (x); 10-25%; 10% or less
Services: Design (x); Landuse planning; Specifications; Installation (x); Site analysis; Maintenance
Specialization: Residential (x); Commercial; Parkland; Corporate grounds; Nature centers; Industrial projects; Roadside

Landescapes
525 S. Flood
Norman, OK 73069
(405)321-2232
Area served: City (x), State, Regional, National
Work with natives: 75-100%; 50-75%; 25-50% (x); 10-25%; 10% or less
Services: Design (x); Landuse planning; Specifications; Installation (x); Site analysis (x); Maintenance (x)
Specialization: Residential (x); Commercial (x); Parkland; Corporate grounds; Nature centers; Industrial projects; Roadside

Emerald Hydro-Turf, Inc.
1840 S.E. 176th
Portland, OR 97233
(503)760-8428 or (503)234-3480
Area served: City, State, Regional (x), National
Work with natives: 75-100%; 50-75%; 25-50%; 10-25%; 10% or less (x)
Services: Design; Landuse planning (x); Specifications (x); Installation (x); Site analysis (x); Maintenance
Specialization: Residential (x); Commercial (x); Parkland (x); Corporate grounds (x); Nature centers (x); Industrial projects (x); Roadside (x)

Oregon Highway Division Landscape Unit
215 Transportation Bldg.
Salem, OR 97310
(503)378-3882
Area served: City, State (x), Regional, National
Work with natives: 75-100%; 50-75%; 25-50% (x); 10-25%; 10% or less
Services: Design (x); Landuse planning; Specifications (x); Installation; Site analysis (x); Maintenance (x)
Specialization: Residential; Commercial; Parkland; Corporate grounds; Nature centers; Industrial projects; Roadside (x)

Andropogon Associates, Ltd.
374 Shurs Lane
Philadelphia, PA 19128
(215)487-0700
Area served: City, State, Regional, National (x)
Work with natives: 75-100% (x); 50-75%; 25-50%; 10-25%; 10% or less
Services: Design (x); Landuse planning (x); Specifications (x); Installation (x); Site analysis (x); Maintenance (x)
Specialization: Residential (x); Commercial (x); Parkland (x); Corporate grounds (x); Nature centers (x); Industrial projects (x); Roadside (x)

FM Mooberry, Consultants
106 Spottswood Lane
Kennett Square, PA 19348
(215)444-5495
Area served: City, State, Regional (x), National
Work with natives: 75-100% (x); 50-75%; 25-50%; 10-25%; 10% or less
Services: Design (x); Landuse planning (x); Specifications; Installation; Site analysis (x); Maintenance (x)
Specialization: Residential; Commercial (x); Parkland (x); Corporate grounds (x); Nature centers (x); Industrial projects; Roadside

Jacobs Ladder Natural Gardens, Inc.
P. O. Box 145
Gladwyne, PA 19035
(215)525-6773
Area served: City, State, Regional (x), National
Work with natives: 75-100% (x); 50-75%; 25-50%; 10-25%; 10% or less
Services: Design (x); Landuse planning (x); Specifications (x); Installation (x); Site analysis (x); Maintenance (x)
Specialization: Residential (x); Commercial; Parkland (x); Corporate grounds; Nature centers (x); Industrial projects; Roadside (x)

Livingston Landscape Architects
1015 Lansing Dr.
Mt. Pleasant, SC 29464
(803)884-6876
Area served: City, State, Regional (x), National
Work with natives: 75-100% (x); 50-75%; 25-50%; 10-25%; 10% or less
Services: Design (x); Landuse planning; Specifications; Installation; Site analysis (x); Maintenance (x)
Specialization: Residential (x); Commercial (x); Parkland (x); Corporate grounds; Nature centers; Industrial projects; Roadside (x)

Cynthia Reed, Consultant
Cascade Ranch
Hot Springs, SD 57747-0461
(605)745-3397
Area served: City, State, Regional (x), National
Work with natives: 75-100% (x); 50-75%; 25-50%; 10-25%; 10% or less
Services: Design; Landuse planning; Specifications; Installation; Site analysis; Maintenance
Specialization: Residential (x); Commercial (x); Parkland (x); Corporate grounds; Nature centers (x); Industrial projects; Roadside

Native Gardens Columbine Farm
Rt. 1 Box 494
Greenback, TN 37742
(615)856-3350
Area served: City, State, Regional (x), National
Work with natives: 75-100% (x); 50-75%; 25-50%; 10-25%; 10% or less
Services: Design; Landuse planning; Specifications; Installation; Site analysis; Maintenance
Specialization: Residential (x); Commercial (x); Parkland; Corporate grounds; Nature centers; Industrial projects (x); Roadside (x)

Anderson Landscape and Nursery
2222 Pech
Houston, TX 77055
(713)984-1342
Area served: City (x), State, Regional, National
Work with natives: 75-100%; 50-75% (x); 25-50%; 10-25%; 10% or less
Services: Design (x); Landuse planning (x); Specifications; Installation (x); Site analysis (x); Maintenance (x)
Specialization: Residential (x); Commercial; Parkland; Corporate grounds; Nature centers; Industrial projects; Roadside

Ben Lednicky & Associates
P. O. Box 770217
Houston, TX 77215
(713)240-7131
Area served: City, State (x), Regional, National
Work with natives: 75-100%; 50-75%; 25-50% (x); 10-25%; 10% or less
Services: Design (x); Landuse planning; Specifications (x); Installation; Site analysis (x); Maintenance (x)
Specialization: Residential (x); Commercial (x); Parkland (x); Corporate grounds (x); Nature centers (x); Industrial projects (x); Roadside (x)

Colorscapes

6105 Mountain Villa Dr.
Austin, TX 78731
(512)451-3379
Area served: City (x), State, Regional, National
Work with natives: 75-100% (x); 50-75%; 25-50%; 10-25%; 10% or less
Services: Design (x); Landuse planning; Specifications; Installation (x); Site analysis; Maintenance
Specialization: Residential (x); Commercial; Parkland; Corporate grounds; Nature centers; Industrial projects; Roadside

Dave Shows and Associates

17320 Classen Rd.
San Antonio, TX 78247
(512)497-3222
Area served: City (x), State, Regional, National
Work with natives: 75-100%; 50-75% (x); 25-50%; 10-25%; 10% or less
Services: Design; Landuse planning; Specifications; Installation; Site analysis; Maintenance
Specialization: Residential (x); Commercial (x); Parkland; Corporate grounds; Nature centers; Industrial projects; Roadside

Dixie Watkins, III

Rt. 3330 Oakwell Court, Suite 110
San Antonio, TX 78218
(512)824-7836
Area served: City (x), State (x), Regional, National
Work with natives: 75-100%; 50-75%; 25-50% (x); 10-25%; 10% or less
Services: Design (x); Landuse planning (x); Specifications (x); Installation; Site analysis (x); Maintenance
Specialization: Residential (x); Commercial (x); Parkland (x); Corporate grounds; Nature centers (x); Industrial projects; Roadside (x)

Dodd Family Tree Nursery and Florist
515 W. Main
Fredericksburg, TX 78624
(512)997-9571
Area served: City (x), State, Regional (x), National
Work with natives: 75-100%; 50-75%; 25-50% (x); 10-25%; 10% or less
Services: Design (x); Landuse planning; Specifications; Installation (x); Site analysis; Maintenance (x)
Specialization: Residential (x); Commercial (x); Parkland; Corporate grounds; Nature centers; Industrial projects; Roadside

Eco-Native Consultants
Rt. 4 Box 366
Bryan, TX 77803
(409)822-4055
Area served: City, State (x), Regional, National
Work with natives: 75-100% (x); 50-75%; 25-50%; 10-25%; 10% or less
Services: Design; Landuse planning; Specifications (x); Installation (x); Site analysis (x); Maintenance (x)
Specialization: Residential; Commercial; Parkland (x); Corporate grounds (x); Nature centers; Industrial projects; Roadside

Environmental Survey Consulting
4602 Placid Place
Austin, TX 78731-5515
(512)458-8531
Area served: City, State, Regional (x), National
Work with natives: 75-100% (x); 50-75%; 25-50%; 10-25%; 10% or less
Services: Design (x); Landuse planning (x); Specifications (x); Installation (x); Site analysis (x); Maintenance (x)
Specialization: Residential (x); Commercial (x); Parkland (x); Corporate grounds (x); Nature centers (x); Industrial projects (x); Roadside (x)

Evergreen Landscape, Inc.
4402 Nixon Lane
Austin, TX 78725
(512)926-9513
Area served: City (x), State (x), Regional, National
Work with natives: 75-100%; 50-75%; 25-50%; 10-25% (x); 10% or less
Services: Design (x); Landuse planning (x); Specifications (x); Installation (x);
Site analysis (x); Maintenance (x)
Specialization: Residential; Commercial (x); Parkland (x); Corporate grounds
(x); Nature centers (x); Industrial projects (x); Roadside

Ford, Powell, and Carson, Inc.
1138 E. Commerce
San Antonio, TX 78205
(512)226-1246
Area served: City, State, Regional (x), National
Work with natives: 75-100%; 50-75%; 25-50% (x); 10-25%; 10% or less
Services: Design (x); Landuse planning (x); Specifications (x); Installation; Site
analysis (x); Maintenance
Specialization: Residential (x); Commercial (x); Parkland (x); Corporate
grounds (x); Nature centers (x); Industrial projects; Roadside

Gardenscapes
703 Meriden Lane
Austin, TX 78703
(512)474-4300
Area served: City (x), State, Regional, National
Work with natives: 75-100% (x); 50-75%; 25-50%; 10-25%; 10% or less
Services: Design (x); Landuse planning; Specifications; Installation (x); Site
analysis (x); Maintenance (x)
Specialization: Residential (x); Commercial; Parkland; Corporate grounds;
Nature centers; Industrial projects; Roadside

J. Robert Anderson, ASLA, Landscape Architect
1135 W. Sixth St., #120
Austin, TX 78703
(512)476-1777
Area served: City (x), State (x), Regional, National
Work with natives: 75-100% (x); 50-75%; 25-50%; 10-25%; 10% or less
Services: Design (x); Landuse planning (x); Specifications (x); Installation; Site analysis (x); Maintenance
Specialization: Residential (x); Commercial (x); Parkland (x); Corporate grounds (x); Nature centers; Industrial projects; Roadside

Johnson Johnson & Roy, Inc.
2828 Routh St., Suite 600
Dallas, TX 75201
(214)871-9220
Area served: City, State, Regional (x), National
Work with natives: 75-100%; 50-75%; 25-50%; 10-25%; 10% or less (x)
Services: Design (x); Landuse planning (x); Specifications (x); Installation; Site analysis (x); Maintenance
Specialization: Residential; Commercial (x); Parkland (x); Corporate grounds (x); Nature centers; Industrial projects; Roadside

McKinnon Associates
831 Cortlandt
Houston, TX 77007
(713)869-2797
Area served: City (x), State, Regional, National
Work with natives: 75-100% (x); 50-75%; 25-50%; 10-25%; 10% or less
Services: Design (x); Landuse planning; Specifications (x); Installation (x); Site analysis (x); Maintenance (x)
Specialization: Residential (x); Commercial (x); Parkland (x); Corporate grounds; Nature centers; Industrial projects; Roadside (x)

Neiman Environments
2088 W. Jeter
Argyle, TX 76226
(214)539-0534
Area served: City, State, Regional (x), National
Work with natives: 75-100% (x); 50-75%; 25-50%; 10-25%; 10% or less
Services: Design (x); Landuse planning (x); Specifications (x); Installation (x); Site analysis (x); Maintenance (x)
Specialization: Residential; Commercial; Parkland (x); Corporate grounds (x); Nature centers (x); Industrial projects (x); Roadside (x)

Personal Ecosystems
712 Keasbey
Austin, TX 78756
(512)453-0564
Area served: City, State (x), Regional, National
Work with natives: 75-100%; 50-75%; 25-50% (x); 10-25%; 10% or less
Services: Design (x); Landuse planning (x); Specifications; Installation (x); Site analysis (x); Maintenance (x)
Specialization: Residential (x); Commercial (x); Parkland; Corporate grounds; Nature centers; Industrial projects; Roadside

Planning Naturally, by Design
P. O. Box 162076
Austin, TX 78716-2076
(512)447-4488
Area served: City (x), State, Regional, National
Work with natives: 75-100% (x); 50-75%; 25-50%; 10-25%; 10% or less
Services: Design (x); Landuse planning (x); Specifications; Installation; Site analysis (x); Maintenance
Specialization: Residential; Commercial; Parkland (x); Corporate grounds; Nature centers (x); Industrial projects; Roadside (x)

Sally Wasowski, Landscape Designer
7241 Westlake
Dallas, TX 75214
(214)327-6220
Area served: City, State (x), Regional, National
Work with natives: 75-100% (x); 50-75%; 25-50%; 10-25%; 10% or less
Services: Design; Landuse planning; Specifications; Installation; Site analysis;
Maintenance
Specialization: Residential (x); Commercial; Parkland (x); Corporate grounds;
Nature centers; Industrial projects; Roadside

Stephen F. Austin State University
Political Science and Geography
SFA Station, P. O. Box 13045
Nacogdoches, TX 75962-3045
(409)568-3903
Area served: City, State, Regional (x), National
Work with natives: 75-100%; 50-75%; 25-50%; 10-25% (x); 10% or less
Services: Design (x); Landuse planning; Specifications; Installation; Site analy-
sis; Maintenance
Specialization: Residential (x); Commercial; Parkland; Corporate grounds;
Nature centers; Industrial projects; Roadside

Stephen K. Domigan
609B W. 32nd St.
Austin, TX 78705-2219
(512)453-5545
Area served: City, State, Regional (x), National
Work with natives: 75-100% (x); 50-75%; 25-50%; 10-25%; 10% or less
Services: Design (x); Landuse planning; Specifications (x); Installation; Site
analysis (x); Maintenance
Specialization: Residential (x); Commercial (x); Parkland; Corporate grounds
(x); Nature centers; Industrial projects; Roadside

Tex-Scape Designs
800 Roaming Rd.
Allen, TX 75002
(214)727-4047
Area served: City (x), State, Regional, National
Work with natives: 75-100%; 50-75% (x); 25-50%; 10-25%; 10% or less
Services: Design (x); Landuse planning; Specifications; Installation; Site analysis; Maintenance
Specialization: Residential (x); Commercial; Parkland; Corporate grounds; Nature centers; Industrial projects; Roadside

Texas Mountain Flora
810 Campbell St.
Lockhart, TX 78644
(512)398-9451
Area served: City (x), State, Regional, National
Work with natives: 75-100%; 50-75% (x); 25-50%; 10-25%; 10% or less
Services: Design; Landuse planning; Specifications; Installation; Site analysis; Maintenance
Specialization: Residential (x); Commercial; Parkland; Corporate grounds; Nature centers (x); Industrial projects; Roadside

Turfmasters Hydromulch
P. O. Box 5311
Jonestown, TX 78645
(512)267-3446 or (512)335-9614
Area served: City (x), State (x), Regional (x), National
Work with natives: 75-100%; 50-75%; 25-50% (x); 10-25%; 10% or less
Services: Design (x); Landuse planning (x); Specifications; Installation (x); Site analysis (x); Maintenance
Specialization: Residential (x); Commercial (x); Parkland (x); Corporate grounds (x); Nature centers (x); Industrial projects (x); Roadside (x)

Waldi Browning, Browning & Associates
2701 Pecos St.
Austin, TX 78703
(512)452-4850
Area served: City (x), State, Regional, National
Work with natives: 75-100% (x); 50-75%; 25-50%; 10-25%; 10% or less
Services: Design (x); Landuse planning; Specifications; Installation (x); Site analysis (x); Maintenance (x)
Specialization: Residential (x); Commercial; Parkland; Corporate grounds; Nature centers; Industrial projects; Roadside

Woodland Plants
3013 Brothers Blvd.
College Station, TX 77845
(409)693-0897
Area served: City (x), State, Regional, National
Work with natives: 75-100% (x); 50-75%; 25-50%; 10-25%; 10% or less
Services: Design (x); Landuse planning; Specifications; Installation (x); Site analysis (x); Maintenance
Specialization: Residential (x); Commercial; Parkland; Corporate grounds; Nature centers; Industrial projects; Roadside

Landmark Design, Inc.
444 S. 300 W, Suite 120
Salt Lake City, UT 84101
(801)363-3500
Area served: City, State (x), Regional, National
Work with natives: 75-100% (x); 50-75%; 25-50%; 10-25%; 10% or less
Services: Design (x); Landuse planning (x); Specifications (x); Installation; Site analysis (x); Maintenance
Specialization: Residential (x); Commercial (x); Parkland (x); Corporate grounds; Nature centers; Industrial projects (x); Roadside (x)

Frosty Hollow
P. O. Box 53
Langley, WA 98260
(206)221-2332
Area served: City, State, Regional (x), National
Work with natives: 75-100% (x); 50-75%; 25-50%; 10-25%; 10% or less
Services: Design; Landuse planning; Specifications; Installation; Site analysis; Maintenance
Specialization: Residential; Commercial; Parkland (x); Corporate grounds; Nature centers (x); Industrial projects (x); Roadside (x)

Lankford Associates
2724 N.E. 55th
Seattle, WA 98105
(206)365-5359
Area served: City (x), State (x), Regional, National
Work with natives: 75-100%; 50-75% (x); 25-50% (x); 10-25%; 10% or less
Services: Design (x); Landuse planning (x); Specifications (x); Installation; Site analysis (x); Maintenance (x)
Specialization: Residential (x); Commercial; Parkland (x); Corporate grounds; Nature centers (x); Industrial projects (x); Roadside (x)

Surroundings
382 Catherine
Walla Walla, WA 99362
(509)525-1126
Area served: City (x), State, Regional (x), National
Work with natives: 75-100%; 50-75%; 25-50%; 10-25% (x); 10% or less
Services: Design (x); Landuse planning; Specifications; Installation (x); Site analysis; Maintenance (x)
Specialization: Residential (x); Commercial; Parkland; Corporate grounds; Nature centers; Industrial projects; Roadside

CRM Ecosystems, Inc.
9738 Overland Rd.
Mt. Horeb, WI 53572
(608)437-5245
Area served: City, State, Regional (x), National
Work with natives: 75-100% (x); 50-75%; 25-50%; 10-25%; 10% or less
Services: Design (x); Landuse planning (x); Specifications (x); Installation (x); Site analysis (x); Maintenance (x)
Specialization: Residential (x); Commercial (x); Parkland; Corporate grounds (x); Nature centers; Industrial projects (x); Roadside

David J. Frank Landscape Contracting, Inc.
P. O. Box 70
N120 W21350 Freistadt Rd.
Germantown, WI 53022
(414)251-0107
Area served: City (x), State, Regional, National
Work with natives: 75-100%; 50-75%; 25-50% (x); 10-25%; 10% or less
Services: Design (x); Landuse planning; Specifications (x); Installation (x); Site analysis (x); Maintenance (x)
Specialization: Residential (x); Commercial (x); Parkland; Corporate grounds (x); Nature centers; Industrial projects; Roadside

Ecoscape
2702 N. 45th St.
Milwaukee, WI 53210
(414)444-3200
Area served: City (x), State, Regional, National
Work with natives: 75-100% (x); 50-75%; 25-50%; 10-25%; 10% or less
Services: Design (x); Landuse planning (x); Specifications; Installation (x); Site analysis (x); Maintenance (x)
Specialization: Residential (x); Commercial; Parkland; Corporate grounds; Nature centers; Industrial projects; Roadside

Judith Z. Stark, ASLA
5438 N. Pauline's Wood Rd.
Nashotah, WI 53058
(414)367-6374
Area served: City, State (x), Regional, National
Work with natives: 75-100%; 50-75%; 25-50%; 10-25% (x); 10% or less
Services: Design (x); Landuse planning (x); Specifications (x); Installation; Site analysis (x); Maintenance
Specialization: Residential (x); Commercial; Parkland; Corporate grounds; Nature centers; Industrial projects; Roadside

LanDesign
P. O. Box 789
Menomonee Falls, WI 53052
(414)251-3883
Area served: City (x), State, Regional, National
Work with natives: 75-100%; 50-75%; 25-50%; 10-25%; 10% or less (x)
Services: Design (x); Landuse planning; Specifications; Installation (x); Site analysis (x); Maintenance
Specialization: Residential (x); Commercial; Parkland; Corporate grounds; Nature centers; Industrial projects; Roadside

Prairie Nursery
P. O. Box 306
Westfield, WI 53964
(608)296-3679
Area served: City, State, Regional (x), National
Work with natives: 75-100% (x); 50-75%; 25-50%; 10-25%; 10% or less
Services: Design (x); Landuse planning (x); Specifications; Installation (x); Site analysis (x); Maintenance
Specialization: Residential (x); Commercial (x); Parkland (x); Corporate grounds (x); Nature centers; Industrial projects; Roadside

Painted Images
Rt. 3 Box 335
Harpers Ferry, WV 25425-9715
(304)535-2235
Area served: City, State, Regional (x), National
Work with natives: 75-100%; 50-75%; 25-50% (x); 10-25%; 10% or less
Services: Design (x); Landuse planning (x); Specifications; Installation; Site analysis (x); Maintenance
Specialization: Residential (x); Commercial (x); Parkland; Corporate grounds; Nature centers; Industrial projects; Roadside